W9-BSV-649

JERRY GARCIA

Recent Titles in Greenwood Biographies

JERRY GARCIA

A Biography

Jacqueline Edmondson

GREENWOOD BIOGRAPHIES

GREENWOOD PRESS
WESTPORT, CONNECTICUT • LONDON

Library of Congress Cataloging-in-Publication Data

Edmondson, Jacqueline, 1967–
  Jerry Garcia : a biography / Jacqueline Edmondson.
    p. cm. — (Greenwood biographies, ISSN 1540–4900)
  Includes bibliographical references and index.
  ISBN 978–0–313–35121–1 (alk. paper)
  1. Garcia, Jerry, 1942–1995. 2. Rock musicians—United States—
Biography. 3. Grateful Dead (Musical group) I. Title.
  ML419.G36E36 2009
  782.42166092—dc22
  [B]   2009005810

British Library Cataloguing in Publication Data is available.

Library of Congress Catalog Card Number: 2009005810

ISBN: 978–0–313–35121–1
ISSN: 1540–4900

First published in 2009

Greenwood Press, 88 Post Road West, Westport, CT 06881
An imprint of Greenwood Publishing Group, Inc.
www.greenwood.com

Printed in the United States of America

The paper used in this book complies with the
Permanent Paper Standard issued by the National
Information Standards Organization (Z39.48–1984).

10 9 8 7 6 5 4 3 2 1

For Michael, Jacob, and Luke

CONTENTS

Photo essay follows page 72

SERIES FOREWORD

In response to high school and public library needs, Greenwood developed this distinguished series of full-length biographies specifically for student use. Prepared by field experts and professionals, these engaging biographies are tailored for high school students who need challenging yet accessible biographies. Ideal for secondary school assignments, the length, format and subject areas are designed to meet educators' requirements and students' interests.

Greenwood offers an extensive selection of biographies spanning all curriculum-related subject areas including social studies, the sciences, literature and the arts, history and politics, as well as popular culture, covering public figures and famous personalities from all time periods and backgrounds, both historic and contemporary, who have made an impact on American and/or world culture. Greenwood biographies were chosen based on comprehensive feedback from librarians and educators. Consideration was given to both curriculum relevance and inherent interest. The result is an intriguing mix of the well known and the unexpected, the saints and sinners from long-ago history and contemporary pop culture. Readers will find a wide array of subject choices from fascinating crime figures like Al Capone to inspiring pioneers like Margaret Mead, from the greatest minds of our time like Stephen Hawking to the most amazing success stories of our day like J. K. Rowling.

While the emphasis is on fact, not glorification, the books are meant to be fun to read. Each volume provides in-depth information about the subject's life from birth through childhood, the teen years, and adulthood.

A thorough account relates family background and education, traces personal and professional influences, and explores struggles, accomplishments, and contributions. A timeline highlights the most significant life events against a historical perspective. Bibliographies supplement the reference value of each volume.

INTRODUCTION

You need music, I don't know why. . . . We need magic, and bliss, and power, myth, and celebration and religion in our lives, and music is a good way to encapsulate a lot of it.

—*Jerry Garcia*

Guitar players strive to create a sound that is uniquely their own. Jerry Garcia was no exception. Garcia's tone and style was so distinctive that some people claim they need to hear only one note to recognize that Jerry is playing. While that claim might seem a bit overstated, listeners surely would be able to distinguish Garcia's style from another guitar player within a short phrase or two. Garcia's approach to music, whether he was playing the acoustic guitar, an electric guitar, a banjo, or a steel guitar, reflected influences from many styles and forms of music. Among them were early American music, bluegrass, blues, country and western, and jazz. Jerry Garcia was most interested in the feelings that he could evoke in his listeners through the music he created. He once described his style by saying, "I really like a clear note, I like syncopations where I can get them in, and I like longer ideas. I think of myself as musically conservative, even though I don't play that way very much. What I like about music is simplicity. It's hard to let something be simple. There's kind of a fear of silence."[1]

Sound was critically important to Garcia. He once commented that he had a memory for sounds, that a sound could transport him to a different place.[2] Because of this, Garcia experimented with sound throughout his life. He played banjos, slide guitars, acoustic guitars, and electric guitars rigged with a variety of knobs and wah-wah pedals. Garcia also enjoyed the variety of digital sounds and computerized technologies that evolved rapidly through the 1970s into the 1990s. Indeed, advances in technology across his lifetime provided Garcia opportunities to manipulate and experiment with different properties of sound: wavelengths, frequencies, amplitudes, and more. From the Grateful Dead's famous "Wall of Sound," the massive amplification system constructed by Owsley Stanley in the 1973, to the more intimate acoustic dynamics in smaller theaters such as San Francisco's Orpheum Theatre, Garcia loved to share different experiences with and through sound with his audiences.

Few would question that Garcia was an impressive and versatile musician. Phil Lesh, bass player for the Grateful Dead, recalled the first time he heard Jerry play:

> I noticed Jerry's distinctive sound the first time we played together. He was playing a Guild Starfire hollowbody, and it had this amazing "spangly" sound—not like a Stratocaster, more bell-like than that. It was almost like he was playing an electric banjo. I was also amazed at his fluency. He was using a banjo fingerpicking technique on some songs, and, on other songs, he'd play with a flatpick. He had all this texture going on, and he sometimes used that in his leads, rather than relying on screaming melodies and big solo flourishes with lots of fast notes.[3]

This artistry, coupled with Garcia's sheer passion for music, brought music lovers from all walks of life to his concerts, whether he was playing for the rock band the Grateful Dead, his bluegrass band Old and in the Way, the blues-style Jerry Garcia Band, or the country-rock group New Riders of the Purple Sage.

Garcia's passion for sound also had what Grateful Dead drummer Mickey Hart later described as a synesthetic effect on Jerry's visual art. Hart explained how "sound evoked colors and colors translated themselves into sound in Garcia's work. It was a kind of silent game he played in his mind."[4] Just as he enjoyed musical colors and tones, Garcia enjoyed visual colors and tones in the oil, watercolor, and even black and white paintings and drawings that were so much a part of his creative world. Some of his art was playful, humorous, and even cartoonlike, while others were more serious, pensive, beautiful, or dark. Garcia engaged the range of visual art in the way he embraced a range of music, always improvising, always creative, and most typically outside the mainstream.

CONTEXTS

When I started the research for this book, *Rolling Stone* magazine was commemorating its 40th anniversary. The July 2007 issue featured a list of 40 essential albums of 1967, the Summer of Love. Included among the titles were: The Beatles' *Sgt. Pepper's Lonely Hearts Club Band* (Capitol), Arlo Guthrie's *Alice's Restaurant* (Reprise), Jefferson Airplane's *Surrealistic Pillow* (RCA), The Doors' *Strange Days* (Elektra), Donovan's *Mellow Yellow* (Epic), Big Brother and the Holding Company's *Big Brother and the Holding Company* (Mainstream), Pink Floyd's *The Piper at the Gates of Dawn* (Columbia), Jimi Hendrix's *Axis: Bold as Love* (Track), the Rolling Stones' *Between the Buttons* (London) and *Flower* (London), The Velvet Underground's *The Velvet Underground and Nico* (Verve), and not surprisingly the Grateful Dead's first album, *The Grateful Dead* (Warner Bros.). The popular music scene in 1967 was bursting with creative energy and innovation, and Garcia's hometown of San Francisco was a hotbed of new music acts, fueled in part by psychedelic drugs, social discontent, and an underlying spirit of anarchy. Jerry Garcia was in the midst of these influences, helping to define the era in unique and specific ways. By 1967, Garcia was already recognized as one of the best guitar players in the country. In addition to his very public presence in the Grateful Dead, Garcia contributed in significant yet sometimes subtle ways to the San Francisco music scene in the 1960s. For example, he had a hand in helping to create a number of albums on *Rolling Stone*'s top 40 list, including Jefferson Airplane's *Surrealistic Pillow*. Garcia can be heard playing guitar on the songs "Today," "Comin' Back to Me," "My Best Friend," and "Plastic Fantastic Lover." Garcia was also close personal friends with many of the artists at this time, including Janis Joplin, David Crosby, Jorma Kaukonen, David Freiberg, and others. The time he spent interacting with these musicians in San Francisco in the 1960s synergistically brought him deeper and more complex understandings of music.

Jerry Garcia's lifestyle was complex and controversial. It is impossible to discuss Garcia's life and music without considering the influence and role of drugs and drug abuse. Garcia began to smoke marijuana when he was 15 years of age, and his involvement with psychedelic drugs began in the mid 1960s with the Acid Tests in La Honda, California. From the 1970s through the time of his death in 1995, Garcia struggled with addictions to heroin and cocaine, habits that made him at times turn toward an increasingly reclusive and isolated way of life. These are not always easy or pleasant aspects of Garcia's life to consider, but at the same time, these influences cannot be ignored. Drugs were integral to the music scene that Jerry Garcia lived, and they were part of his life on and off the stage.

Many people have tried to determine why Jerry became so dependent on drugs. Some suggest that he had an addictive personality, while others believe his anarchist views meant he believed he could do whatever he wanted. His second wife, Mountain Girl, offered a different possibility. She suggested that Jerry understood that the moment between waking and sleeping was a particularly creative space, and that he was continually striving to reach this place to push the boundaries of his creativity.[5] Jerry did not offer many insights about his drug abuse, and so we are left to wonder about this.

In addition to struggling with drug addictions, Garcia's life was fraught with other personal challenges. He was married three times, and he had several serious as well as some fleeting relationships with women. He was father to four daughters with three different women, although his touring schedule made it difficult for him to spend much time with any of them. Garcia allowed nearly two decades to pass without seeing his oldest daughter Heather, who was born in 1963. And although he tried to be more involved with his youngest daughter, Keelin, born in 1987, Garcia was drawn away from her as he continued to tour and become involved in relationships that distanced him from Keelin's mother Manasha.

Most complicated perhaps was that Garcia was viewed as the leader of the Grateful Dead and felt the burden of this responsibility, particularly after the Grateful Dead became an industry that supported so many people and their families. Garcia never really wanted to be a leader; instead, he just wanted to play music, and he hoped someone would want to listen. In 1972, he explained:

> I'm not the leader of the Grateful Dead or anything like that . . . because I can bullshit you guys real easy, but I can't bullshit Phil or Pigpen and them guys watchin' me go through my changes all these years, and we've had so many weird times together . . . I know in front, the leader doesn't work because you don't need one.[6]

Garcia's style was to seek shared decisions among his band mates and friends, and he did not try to impose his own beliefs on others. This applied not just to the musicians in the band, but also to the crew who worked to set up the stage, run the lights and sound, and care for the instruments. The Dead had a uniquely egalitarian relationship with all who were integral to the group, including musicians, road crew, and staff. Yet some critics explained that the idea of the Grateful Dead as a democracy really was a myth; instead, the Grateful Dead "has been and always will be

Jerry Garcia."[7] In spite of this, however, people sought Garcia out for his opinion about many issues, and while Garcia resented his celebrity and generally did not like to deal with unpleasant situations, he was gracious to those who seemed to need his advice or opinion, and he had a tremendous impact at a personal level on many people.

Jerry Garcia fans are found in all walks of life and come from wide yet sometimes improbable circles. Often people think of Garcia's fans as hippies dressed in tie-dyed clothes with bare feet, flowers, and long hair, but conservative pundits like Tucker Carlson, Deroy Murdock, and Ann Coulter also claim to be Grateful Dead fans. They link their appreciation for Jerry Garcia to perceived similarities they find between Garcia's philosophy and that of Ronald Reagan and traditional conservative principles.[8] While this may be a stretch for those who know and understand Garcia's work and philosophies on life, it is worth noting that the Dead's outdoor concerts were often performed with an American flag as a backdrop, and the themes and forms of many of their songs are distinctly American, reflecting old-time American music and stories.

As I worked on this book, I met many people who felt a personal connection to Jerry Garcia, even though he had been dead for more than 12 years. People willingly shared their stories about Garcia with me. One person told me how he lived in San Francisco when Garcia was in a coma and how that made headlines in the *San Francisco Chronicle*, something that seemed to be an irony at the time since Garcia was not considered to be part of the mainstream establishment. A cab driver in Palo Alto told me about his brother's friendship with Pigpen's brother, and how the two young men listened to the Warlocks when they were still basically a garage band struggling to find a good sound. A waiter at St. Michael's Alley proudly shared stories about the Dead playing the venue, along with Jefferson Airplane, Joan Baez, and other big acts of the 1960s. The restaurant is now relocated a few blocks from its original space and under new ownership, but there is still a sense of pride in the musical legacy attached to the name. Most often, people shared their personal experiences attending Grateful Dead concerts, both positive and negative. Some loved being part of the Deadhead scene, while others complained that the music really was not that great. Several people talked of their interest in Garcia's bluegrass music, and one person told me about bumping into Garcia backstage at a concert where he was greeted by the legend with a smile and a short guitar riff.

Young people continue to listen to Garcia's music and know of his connections not just to the Grateful Dead but also to David Grisman and Garcia's other bands. Some of these young people grew up with their parents listening to Garcia's music, while others seemed to find it on their own. One young person shared with me: "I love Garcia's music. You can listen to it any time—when you are riding in the car, going to sleep, whatever. It is just great music."

Jerry Garcia's legacy to American culture is unquestionable. Garcia's music and his approach to the music industry had an enormous impact that remains today. The Grateful Dead focused primarily on live shows, and its members were suspicious of the record industry, particularly in the band's early days. Garcia and his band mates felt that music should be freely shared, and they encouraged fans to record and distribute performances. The Dead even set up special sections of the amphitheater for those who wished to make taped recordings because they felt it would contribute to their success as a band.[9] Of course this was well before the time of file-sharing through Napster, Bear Share, or other internet forums, and some see Garcia and his band mates as prescient in this regard.

Garcia is perhaps one of the most recorded guitar players in history.[10] There are thousands of hours of recordings of his music captured in the 2,200 Grateful Dead concerts, the 1,000 Jerry Garcia Band concerts, and more. Recent new releases of his music in *The Very Best of Jerry Garcia* (2006) and *Pure Jerry* (2006) are reminders of the tremendous range, discipline, and talent that Garcia brought to his craft. Bob Weir, Phil Lesh, and others keep Garcia's music in front of live audiences (see Appendix 1 for current information on the members of the Grateful Dead and others who were close to Jerry). Guitarist Trey Anastasio of Phish credits Garcia as one of the primary influences on his guitar style.

In addition to the music legacy, Garcia's work as a visual artist is becoming increasingly well known. Garcia's paintings, drawings, and sketchbooks are of wide public interest, and some have been published in books, while others can be seen in exhibits or on Web sites. The books *Jerry Garcia: The Collected Artwork* and *J. Garcia: Paintings, Drawings and Sketches* have wonderful collections of some of Garcia's visual art, along with some stories about the contexts in which some pieces were created. These texts show the range of his visual work, from cartoonlike sketches of people and spaceships to watercolor, air-brush pieces, darker work with ink, and some pieces created using technology on a Macintosh computer.

A WORD ON SOURCES

As I worked on this book, several sources were indispensable and are worth noting at the outset. Blair Jackson's biography *Garcia: An American Life* (1999) is probably the most thorough biography on Garcia's life I read, and it was indispensable to this project. Jackson focused primarily on the creative contributions Garcia made to the world of music, and for readers who wish to better understand this aspect of Garcia's impact on American music and culture, I highly recommend this book. In many ways, it makes sense that Jackson would write a comprehensive biography on Garcia. Jackson was a Grateful Dead fan, attending more than 350 Grateful Dead concerns over a 25-year period, and he followed Garcia's life across the course of his career. Jackson had a reputation as a prolific writer, with the Grateful Dead being his favorite subject. Information from more than 150 interviews, including 9 with Garcia, is incorporated into Jackson's book. Jackson has an extensive Web site where interview quotes and other information that was not included in his book is made public.

Dennis McNally's biography of the Grateful Dead, *A Long Strange Trip*, is considered to be a classic. McNally, who was the public relations manager for the Grateful Dead, is often referred to as the official historian for the band, and his writing about the Grateful Dead provided a great deal of information for this book. I was not able to provide detailed accounts of every aspect of the Grateful Dead's touring and various escapades because to do so would be beyond the scope of this book; however, for those readers interested in more in-depth accounts of the band's experiences, I highly recommend this book. McNally's accounts of Garcia's life and experiences were highly consistent with Jackson's, and both authors provided excellent sources for this book.

Robert Greenfield's book *Dark Star* is a series of oral accounts from people close to Garcia, along with excerpts of interviews Garcia gave over the years of his music career. This book provided a great deal of information about Jerry's drug use and health problems because the sources were quite close to Garcia, including Dr. Randy Baker and Yen-Wei Choong who both treated Jerry for health issues during the final years of his life. Similarly the book *Garcia: A Signpost to a New Space* contains lengthy interviews and conversations between Garcia, Charles Reich, and Jann Wenner, a reporter who interviewed Garcia during his early days with the Grateful Dead. Finally, Jerry Garcia engaged in numerous interviews with the staff of *Rolling Stone* magazine over the many years of his music career. He loved to talk, and many of these interviews contain long stretches where Jerry is answering a question or elaborating on something that happened. He explained to Charles Reich in one of these interviews:

> Here's the thing . . . I'm one of those guys who's a compulsive question answerer. But that doesn't necessarily mean I'm right or anything. That's just one of the things I can do. It's kinda like having a trick memory. I can answer any question. I'm just the guy who found myself in the place of doing the talking every time there was an interview with the Grateful Dead.[11]

These interviews were compiled posthumously in *Garcia: By the Editors of the Rolling Stone* (1995), a collection that also included tributes to Garcia, edited by Holly George-Warren. The compilation provided opportunities to insert Garcia's own language and voice into this book.

Several television specials, Internet sources, and films document different aspects of Garcia's life. The VH1 broadcast of the Classic Album Series titled *The Grateful Dead: Anthem to Beauty* offers a wonderful discussion of the band's early efforts to capture their music in a studio.[12] A combination of interviews, video, and photographs, the documentary provides insight into the band's process when working on *Anthem of the Sun, American Beauty*, and *Workingman's Dead*. YouTube houses numerous clips of Jerry Garcia playing with the Grateful Dead and other bands, as well as clips from television interviews, *Saturday Night Live* performances, and other random moments (for example, playing in the parking lot at Woodstock). These clips provide an interesting mosaic of Garcia's life. Finally, several films capture Garcia's performances and personality. *Grateful Dawg* has clips of Garcia playing with friend David Grisman along with a number of interviews with friends and colleagues. *Grateful Dead: The Closing of the Winterland* is one of several films that feature the band during live performances. Anyone interested in Jerry's music should watch the many recorded live performances of the Grateful Dead.

Jerry Garcia's autobiographical book *Harrington Street* (1995) is a provocative personal account of Garcia's life up to the age of 10. A mixture of sketches, paintings, and hand-written notes using mixtures of print and calligraphy along with typed text, the book reveals the pain, struggles, and hopes Garcia felt as a child. Deborah Koons Garcia, Jerry's wife at the time he was writing this book, revealed that he worked on this text nearly every day for 18 months, that it "came from his heart and helped him heal his heart."[13] Jerry described the book and his writing process:

> It's AUTO-APOCRYPHA, full of my ANECDOUBTS. Like things to do with my relatives, my family, the block I grew up on, the things that scared me (animals), the discovery of fire, you know, things like that. I've written to age 10. I talk to myself, sort of remember things about my family, things they told me, things I think I heard. Then I wonder how I picked up that information, as it seems so familiar. But then it is twisted through my own imagination, which is warped. I write the text out longhand, but my drawings, which illustrate my text, I do on computer. I'm taking it totally free, it's really FUN!

I'm pleased with what I am doing. The look is so unique—it
doesn't look like anything else I have ever seen!!!![14]

Although the book was not in print until after Jerry died, all but two
childhood stories are told through his actual writing.

Titles for each of the chapters in this book, along with the subheadings
in the chapters, come from song lyrics that Garcia performed across his
career. A complete list of these lyrics can be found at Grateful Dead Lyrics.[15] Finally, a list of the guitars Garcia used across his career can be found
in Appendix 2.

Many books, articles, films, and Web sites have been dedicated to telling
Garcia's story. The purpose of this biography is to synthesize these numerous sources into an interesting and comprehensive yet concise account of
Garcia's life that will spark interest among readers and lead them to these
other sources and further research. To contribute to this goal, a brief timeline captures some of the key events in Garcia's life, along with highlights
of various U.S. and world events that occurred across the course of his
lifetime. The appendices provide further information about Garcia's band
mates, guitars, and music. The glossary is a resources to help explain some
of the key people, groups, events, and terms used in the book. My hope is
that readers will come to appreciate Jerry Garcia's unique and longstanding contributions to American culture, and that these understandings will
contribute to a deeper sense of American life and history.

NOTES

1. Jon Sievert, "Remembering the Music, Vibe, and Guitars of Jerry Garcia,"
Guitar Player: Online Edition, http://www.guitarplayer.com/article/remembering-
the-music/Nov-05/15094 (accessed November 21, 2008).

2. Blair Jackson, *Garcia: An American Life*. New York: The Penguin Group,
1999.

3. Sievert, "Remembering the Music . . ."

4. April Higashi, *Jerry Garcia: The Collected Artwork*. New York: Thunders
Mouth Press, 2005, p. xi.

5. Robert Greenfield, *Dark Star*. New York: William Morrow and Company,
1996.

6. Holly George-Warren, *Garcia: By the Editors of The Rolling Stone*. New York:
Little Brown and Company, 1995, p. 46.

7. John Rocco, *Dead Reckonings: The Life and Times of the Grateful Dead*. New
York: Schirmer Books, 1999, p. 102.

8. *The New York Sun*, http://www.nysun.com/article/18288 (accessed November 21, 2008).

9. Seth Schiesel, "Jerry Garcia: The Man, the Myth, the Area Rug," *The New York Times*, http://www.nytimes.com/2005/08/09/national/09dead.html (accessed November 21, 2008).

10. Henry Kaiser, "Jerry Garcia Live!," *Guitar Player: Online Edition*, http://www.guitarplayer.com/article/jerry-garcia-live/oct-07/32077 (accessed November 21, 2008).

11. George-Warren, p. 88.

12. Jeremy Marre, *The Grateful Dead: Anthem to Beauty*. New York: Eagle Rock Entertainment, 1997.

13. Jerry Garcia, *Harrington Street*. New York: Delacourt Press, 1995, n.p.

14. Ibid.

15. "Grateful Dead Lyrics," http://www.cs.cmu.edu/~mleone/dead-lyrics.html (accessed November 21, 2008).

ACKNOWLEDGMENTS

I would like to give special thanks to Patrick Shannon, Murry Nelson, and Jeremy Cohen for discussions of this book and for reading earlier drafts. I would also like to thank Alexandra D'Urso, my research assistant, for her careful work and enthusiasm.

As always, my deepest appreciation goes to my husband, Michael, and our sons, Jacob and Luke, for their love and support as I worked on this book. As I began this project, I had many questions about how to handle the more sensitive topics related to Jerry Garcia's life, particularly the drug abuse. It was Jacob, who was 15 years old at the time, who assured me that I must write about it all because that is what he and his friends would want to know. He quickly followed this statement with the reminder that I also needed to write about why Garcia died at such a young age, his acknowledgment of the devastating effects drug abuse brings. Jacob believes, and I agree, that we must be straightforward with young people about what happens in the world and among people so that younger generations can make better decisions than those before them have. Annabelle Garcia McLean, Jerry's daughter, confirmed that this is possible in an interview she gave to Donna Horowitz of the *San Francisco Examiner* in 1996. She recalled that Jerry used to tell her and her sisters,

> "You kids should do drugs."
>
> It was sort of a running family joke . . . her mother would also say: "Why can't you kids be more like us?" We'd tell her, "Mom, no, we don't want to. We learned from you guys."[1]

NOTE

1. Donna Horowitz, "Daddy Garcia," *SF Gate*, http://www.sfchroniclemarket-place.com/cgi-bin/article.cgi?f=/e/a/1996/12/26/NEWS9534.dtl&hw=annabelle+garcia&sn=007&sc=589 (accessed November 21, 2008).

TIMELINE: EVENTS IN THE LIFE OF JERRY GARCIA

1934 Jerry Garcia's parents, Joe Garcia and Ruth Marie Clifford, meet. They marry the following year on April 29, 1935.

1937 Joe Garcia opens Garcia's, a bar/restaurant at the corner of First and Harrison Streets in San Francisco. On December 20, Clifford "Tiff" Garcia is born at Children's Hospital in San Francisco.

1941 The Japanese attack Pearl Harbor on December 7, and the United States enters World War II.

1942 On August 1, Jerome John "Jerry" Garcia is born at Children's Hospital in San Francisco.

1946 The middle finger of Jerry's right hand is cut off while chopping wood with his brother Tiff.

1947 On August 24, Jerry's father Joe drowns while fishing in the Trinity River.

1953 Ruth marries Wadislof "Wally" Matusiewicz in Reno, Nevada.

1955 Beat poet Allen Ginsberg gives his first public reading of the poem *Howl* at the Six Gallery in San Francisco, founded by artist Wally Hedrick. Hedrick would later become Jerry's art teacher. On November 1, President Dwight D. Eisenhower deploys the Military Assistance Advisory Group to Vietnam, marking the official entry of the United States in the Vietnam Conflict.

1956 Jerry watches the movie *Rock around the Clock*, featuring Bill Haley and His Comets. Jerry tells his cousin Daniel that they could play rock that well.

1957 Jerry's mother gives him an accordion for his 15th birthday. They later trade it at a pawnshop for an electric guitar and amplifier.

1958   Jerry begins to take art classes at the California Institute of the Arts (later called the San Francisco Art Institute).

1959   Kurt Vonnegut publishes his second novel, *The Sirens of Titan*, one of Garcia's favorite books. Buddy Holly, Ritchie Valens, and J. P. Richardson (The Big Bopper) die in a plane crash February 3. Jerry drops out of high school.

1960   In February, Jerry's maternal grandfather Pop Clifford dies. On April 12, Jerry enlists in the Army. On October 19, he is convicted for being illegally off base (AWOL or Absent Without Leave). On December 14, Jerry leaves the army.

1961   Ruth and Wally Matusiewicz separate, and Ruth returns to Harrington Street to care for her mother, Tillie. February 20, Jerry survives a serious car accident that kills his friend Paul Speegle.

1962   On February 12, Wally Matusiewicz dies of a massive heart attack while driving Ruth to work. Jerry does not attend the funeral. On May 11, the Thunder Mountain Tub Thumpers opens the Stanford University Folk Festival with Garcia playing guitar. Garcia forms the Sleepy Hollow Hog Stompers with friend Marshall Leicester.

1963   On April 25, Jerry marries Sara Ruppenthal at the Palo Alto Unitarian Church. The United States unsuccessfully attempts to overthrow Cuban President Fidel Castro in the Bay of Pigs.
        In May, the first Monterey Folk Festival is held at the Monterey County Fairgrounds. President John F. Kennedy is assassinated November 22 in Dallas, Texas. On December 8, Jerry and Sara's daughter Heather is born at Stanford Hospital.
        On December 31, Bob Weir and Jerry Garcia discuss forming a band. The Beatles release *Hard Days' Night*.

1964   Jerry travels cross-country with Sandy Rothman and David Nelson as a member of the bluegrass band the Black Mountain Boys. He is unsuccessful getting a gig with Bill Monroe. Garcia returns to San Francisco to form the Asphalt Mountain Jungle Boys with Eric Thompson and Jody Stecher and Mother McCree's Uptown Jug Champions with Bob Weir and Ron McKernan (aka Pigpen). Jerry also plays with an electric blues/rock group called the Zodiacs.

1965   The Warlocks play for *One Flew Over the Cuckoo's Nest* author Ken Kesey's parties, called the Acid Tests. Garcia takes LSD for the first time. The Warlocks become increasingly popular and change their name to the Grateful Dead.

1966   The Grateful Dead become one of the top bands in the Haight-Ashbury district, playing numerous concerts.
        Sunshine Kesey, Ken Kesey and Carolyn "Mountain Girl" Adams's daughter, is born in Mexico. The Dead spend six idyllic weeks at Olompali Ranch in California.

On August 6, John Lennon reports to the press that The Beat-les are "more popular than Jesus." On October 6, California rules that LSD is illegal.

1967 The Grateful Dead play for a crowd of 30,000 at a Human Be-In at Golden Gate Park. Jerry Garcia contributes to Jefferson Air-plane's album *Surrealistic Pillow*, released in February. The Dead sign a record contract with Warner Brothers for $3,500. The album, called *The Grateful Dead*, is released in March. In May, the band travels to New York, playing its first concerts on the east coast. The Summer of Love begins with the Monterey Pop Festi-val. The Beatles release *Revolver* and *Sgt. Pepper's Lonely Heart's Club Band*. Riots break out in Newark, New Jersey and Detroit, Michigan. In July, jazz great Johnny Coltrane dies. In Septem-ber, drummer Mickey Hart joins the Grateful Dead. In October, Woody Guthrie and Che Guevara die, and the antiwar move-ment brings protest marches to Washington, DC.

1968 The Grateful Dead tour extensively, performing in Miami, Phil-adelphia, New York, St. Louis, and Los Angeles. Neal Cassady dies February 4. In March, the band gives its final performance on Haight Street. The Dead's second album, *Anthem of the Sun* (Warner Bros.), is released in July. Recording sessions for their third album begin in September. Mickey and the Hartbeats (the Dead minus Weir and Pigpen) play a few gigs together. Tom Con-stanten joins the Dead on keyboards in November. Martin Luther King, Jr. is assassinated April 4. Robert Kennedy is assassinated June 6.

1969 Garcia continues touring extensively with the Grateful Dead. Lenny Hart, Mickey's dad, becomes manager. The Dead's third album, *Aoxomoxoa* (Warner Bros.), appears in stores in June. Gar-cia picks up a Zane Beck pedal steel guitar and begins to play with John Dawson, David Nelson, Phil Lesh, and Mickey Hart as New Riders of the Purple Sage. The Grateful Dead play at Woodstock in New York. The Rolling Stones play at Altamont, a concert that results in violence and death. In November, the Dead release a live double-LP set called *Live Dead*. Tom Constanten decides to leave the Dead.

1970 The Grateful Dead perform a record 142 shows. Members of the Dead are busted on narcotics charges while touring in New Or-leans. Jerry and Mountain Girl welcome daughter Annabelle. The Dead cut three albums for Warner Bros.: *Live/Dead*, *American Beauty*, and *Workingman's Dead*, which is voted top album of the year by *Rolling Stone* magazine readers. Lenny Hart and Jonathan Reister depart from management positions with the Dead after

Hart's mismanagement and embezzlement is revealed. Sam Cutler and Dave and Bonnie Parker join the management team. Mickey Hart leaves the band.

1971   New Riders of the Purple Sage release their first album; Jerry decides to leave the group. The Grateful Dead release *Grateful Dead* for Warner Bros. Apollo 14 successfully lands on the Moon. Bill Graham closes the Fillmore East in New York City in June.

1972   Jerry's solo album, *Garcia*, is released in January. The Dead tour Europe and release the album *Europe '72* for Warner Bros. In May, President Richard Nixon and Soviet President Leonid Brezhnev sign the first Strategic Arms Limitation Talks Treaty in Moscow.

1973   A peace treaty is signed to end the Vietnam War. On March 8, Pigpen dies from liver problems. Jerry and Mountain Girl watch the Watergate Hearings, which expose political scandals and corruption during Richard Nixon's presidency, on television. The Grateful Dead release an album for Warner Bros., *Bear's Choice*, and start their own record production company, Grateful Dead Records. Their first album under this label, *Wake of the Flood*, is released. The Wall of Sound, a massive speaker system, is created by Owsley Stanley.

1974   Jerry releases his second solo album, also called *Garcia*. The Grateful Dead release *Grateful Dead from the Mars Hotel* and *Skeletons from the Closet*. Richard Nixon is impeached and resigns the presidency on August 9. Gerald Ford is sworn in as U.S. president. The Grateful Dead kick off a short European tour in London in September. They end the year with shows at the Winterland, and then take a hiatus from touring.

1975   *Blues for Allah* is released. Saigon falls, ending the Vietnam War.

1976   The Grateful Dead release *Steal Your Face*. On September 6, longtime Grateful Dead crew member Rex Jackson dies in a car accident.

1977   *Terrapin Station* is released by the Grateful Dead. Apple Computer Inc. is incorporated. Elvis Presley dies on August 16 at 42 years of age.

1978   The Grateful Dead play *Saturday Night Live*. The Grateful Dead perform concerts in front of the Great Pyramids in Egypt. The Camp David Accords are signed on September 17. Cult preacher Jim Jones leads hundreds to their death in Guyana, including many Bay Area residents. Jerry meets Manasha Matheson, and the two later enter a relationship and have a child together. The Dead close the Winterland on December 31. *Shakedown Street* is released by the Grateful Dead. The Jerry Garcia Band releases *Cats under the Stars*.

1979   Donna and Keith Godchaux leave the band. Jerry lives in a rented house in Hepburn Heights in San Rafael.

1980   Keith Godchaux dies in an automobile accident. *Go to Heaven* is released. John Lennon is murdered on December 8.

1981   MTV launches on Jerry's birthday, August 1. The Grateful Dead tour Europe in March and September. Danny Rifkin replaces Richard Loren as the Grateful Dead's manager. *Reckoning* and *Dead Set* are released. Jerry marries Mountain Girl on New Year's Eve.

1982   Jerry's solo album *Run for the Roses* is released.

1983   The Grateful Dead found the Rex Foundation to benefit environmental, human service, and arts groups.

1984   Jerry's drug use worsens and his family and friends attempt to intervene.

1985   On January 18, a day before he was scheduled to enter rehab, Jerry is arrested with 23 packets of heroin and cocaine while sitting in his BMW at Golden Gate Park.

1986   Jerry focuses his time off the road on visual art, and he is clean. After the summer tour, he collapses in a diabetic coma and is hospitalized. He spends the fall recovering and learning to play guitar again.

1987   Jerry tours with Bob Dylan and he performs on Broadway. "Touch of Grey" is a hit on the radio and on MTV. Jerry and girlfriend Manasha Matheson welcome daughter Keelin, yet he remains married to Mountain Girl. Grateful Dead album *In the Dark* reaches the top 10 in the Billboard Hot 100, the highest ranking a Dead album would receive. More than a million copies are sold in the year it is released

1988   The Dead work on the album *Built to Last*. The Soviet Union begins its economic restructuring (perestroika).

1989   Barbara Meier's book of poetry *The Life You Ordered Has Arrived* is published. *Dylan and the Dead* and *Built to Last* are released.

1990   Grateful Dead keyboardist Brett Mydland dies at 37 years of age. *Without a Net* and *Dozin' at the Knick* are released. Jerry asks Manasha to marry him, but the wedding never takes place.

1991   The first Gulf War begins in January and ends in March. Bill Graham dies October 25 in a helicopter crash. *Rolling Stone* magazine votes the album *Aoxomoxoa* as the eighth greatest album cover of all time, and *American Beauty*'s album cover the 57th best of all time. *One from the Vault* and *Infrared Roses* are released.

1992   *Two from the Vault* is released. Jerry moves in with Manasha to be closer to his daughter Keelin.

1993   Jerry leaves Manasha after reuniting with Barbara Meier, but the relationship with Meier, while happy, is short-lived. Jerry visits the White House, meeting Al and Tipper Gore. Jerry travels with Deborah Koons to Ireland in July. Jerry's art show opens in Japan October 20. Jerry's divorce from Mountain Girl is finalized at the end of the year. He marries Deborah Koons three weeks later.

1994   Jerry's performances are uneven as he struggles with drug addiction and carpal tunnel syndrome. He collapses back stage at the Desert Sky Pavilion in Phoenix while performing with The Jerry Garcia Band.

1995   On January 19, Jerry is involved in a serious car accident. On August 9, Garcia dies after checking into the Serenity Knolls rehab center.

1996   On May 30, John Kahn, Garcia's longtime friend and bass player, dies from heart disease.

2002   The remaining members of the Grateful Dead gather at Alpine Valley in Wisconsin, a place they named Terrapin Station. It is the first time they have played an entire show together since Jerry's death.

2003   *Live Dead* ranks 244th, *American Beauty* ranks 258th, *Workingman's Dead* ranks 262nd, and *Anthem of the Sun* ranks 287th on *Rolling Stone*'s list of the top 500 albums ("The RS 500 Greatest Albums of All Time," *Rolling Stone*, http://www.rollingstone.com/news/story/5938174/the_rs_500_greatest_albums_of_all_time/ [accessed November 21, 2008]).

2007   The Grateful Dead are awarded a Grammy Lifetime Achievement Award.

2008   On August 1, Dead Symphony premiered on the sixty-sixth anniversary of Jerry's birthday. Living members of the Grateful Dead reunite to perform several benefit concerts in support of Barack Obama's presidential campaign.

Chapter 1

THE MUSIC NEVER STOPPED: LIFE WITH THE GARCIA AND CLIFFORD FAMILIES

The Excelsior District of San Francisco was certainly an exciting place for a young boy growing up in the 1940s and 1950s. To a rambunctious and fearless child like Jerry Garcia, there would be few places like this city or this neighborhood. The Excelsior District is situated on the southern boundary of San Francisco with a stunning view of the downtown area of the city and the southern hills. Here Jerry could spend his days kicking around town with his brother and his friends, riding bikes or hopping on the back of a trolley for some new adventure.

Excelsior was a working-class neighborhood teeming with Irish, German, Swiss, and other European immigrants. Jerry's own grandparents were immigrants or children of immigrants, contributing to the ethnic, linguistic, and cultural diversity of the community. Jerry's grandfather Manuel Garcia emigrated to the United States from Spain just after World War I. He moved his family from a small fishing community called Sada in the Galicia region of Spain to San Francisco, California because he thought America was a land of opportunity and he would be able to provide his family a better life in the United States. Situated on the northwest corner of the Iberian Peninsula, Sada has a beautiful view of the Ria de Bentanzos, an estuary that is part of the Gulf Artabro. In some ways, the San Francisco Bay Area may have reminded Manuel and his family a little of their former home. Yet the communities were half a world apart, in more ways than one.

In the early 1900s, there were nearly two million people who lived in the Galicia region, but San Francisco had significantly fewer residents, just over 500,000. And while the Sada community was largely homogenous, with people speaking the Galician and Spanish languages, San Francisco had a mixture of European, Japanese, and Chinese immigrants along with African American and native people who spoke a variety of languages and reflected a diversity of cultures.

Manuel was a seaman, and his job took him all over the world. But when Manuel settled in San Francisco in 1918, his livelihood changed. Rather than continuing to work on the ocean, he found employment with the railroad. Manuel applied to become a U.S. citizen almost immediately after he arrived in the city, and later that year, after he had saved some money, Manuel sent for his family to join him. Manuel and his wife Aquilena had four children, all of whom relocated to the United States. Young Manuel was the oldest (b. 1901), named after his father. Jose was just a year younger than his brother. Leonor (b. 1908) and Lena (b. 1912) completed the family.

En route to the United States, Aquilena and the children traveled first to Havana, and then to New York City's Ellis Island to be "processed." Any immigrant who was not wealthy was required to pass rigorous mental and physical examinations in order to be admitted to the country. Aquilena's nephew Atonio Dalmau emigrated with the family; however, he had polio as a child and could not pass the six-second physical examination at Ellis Island. The authorities sent him back home to Spain.[1] After heartbreaking farewells to Atonio, the Garcia family continued their travel by train from New York City to California where they settled in North Beach, a community with many Italian immigrants.

Soon Manuel changed jobs to work as a steam engineer for Pacific Gas & Electric, a position he held for nearly 40 years,[2] and the Garcia family moved to the outer Mission district to a home on Precita Avenue. The city was very segregated, and the neighborhoods reflected the ethnic origin of the residents. The Mission district is one of the oldest in San Francisco, originally home to the Ohlone Indians and later settled by Spanish friars who wished to convert the natives to Catholicism. Largely spared during the 1906 earthquake and fire, the district became home to many working-class people, and the labor movement was quite strong in this region. The Irish were a powerful presence in this neighborhood through the 1930s; but in time, the district became home to many Central American immigrants.

Embracing his new country, Manuel learned English well, something his wife refused to do, and he came to love the United States quite deeply. Manuel was particularly fond of Franklin D. Roosevelt and the New Deal. He seemed to agree with the premise that the federal government should be instrumental in moving the country out of the Great Depression, and he supported the government programs that were put in place to provide jobs for the unemployed.

Manuel's eldest son fared quite well in school, and he became an engineer. Manuel's youngest son, Jose, shared his father's love for the United States, and he decided that he would not speak Spanish as a demonstration of loyalty to his new country. Jose eventually changed his name to Joe, listing his name as "Joseph" on official documents. Joe was much more interested in music than school. Although his father wanted him to become a machinist, Joe preferred to play clarinet and saxophone and hoped to make a career in music. He gave lessons to children in the neighborhood and played jazz and other popular music with different groups in the San Francisco area, including events at the Warfield Theatre and the Orpheum Theatre. Eventually, Joe traveled across the United States as a member of the Orpheum Theatre orchestra, and then he settled in Los Angeles, where he played in a small combo group as well as for an orchestra and a film studio run by Mary Pickford. Joe married a woman named Sunny, but he wished to have a family and Sunny did not.[3] As the marriage ended, Joe returned to the San Francisco area, where he attempted to continue his career as a musician, but he quickly discovered that this was not easy to do. For one, the country was in the midst of the Great Depression and money was tight. Attending live music performances was a luxury not everyone could afford. In addition, the record industry began to change the music world. People began to buy record albums and attend fewer live music events. The final straw came when Joe allowed his orchestra to play for free on the radio and at a nightclub. The union fined him $1,500 and suspended him from work for six months.[4] He decided to leave the music business altogether.

In 1934, Joe met Ruth Marie Clifford, a nurse at the San Francisco General Hospital. The two married on April 29, 1935, and Joe and his business partner opened a bar and restaurant called Garcia's on the corner of First and Harrison Streets, a prime location on the waterfront. There was a hotel upstairs. The business was in a rough neighborhood near the docks, and the clientele was primarily seamen.

Shortly after Garcia's opened, Joe and Ruth welcomed their first child into the family. Clifford Ramon Garcia was born on December 20, 1937. Five years later, on August 1, 1942, Joe and Ruth welcomed their second son, Jerome John Garcia, to the family. Baby Jerome, who became known as Jerry, was presciently named for the musician Jerome Kern (1885–1945), an American composer who wrote over 700 songs in the early 1900s. Kern's music was quite popular in his day, and many of his tunes have become standard classics: "Ol' Man River," "Smoke Gets in Your Eyes," and "The Way You Look Tonight." From a young age, Jerry admired his older brother, whom he called "Tiff," a nickname that stayed throughout his lifetime.

With their two young sons, the Garcia's had many happy times. The young family often spent Sunday afternoons with grandfather Manuel and the other members of the Garcia family where heated discussions of political issues were the norm before dinner, and music and singing were typical after dinner. When they weren't with the Garcias, the young family visited with Ruth's parents, Bill and Tillie Clifford, who lived nearby in the Excelsior district of San Francisco.

Joe and Ruth Garcia's home was always full of music. Although Joe no longer worked as a professional musician, he still played the saxophone and clarinet at home, for family occasions, and in his restaurant for the seamen who would listen. Joe liked swing music that was popular at the time, including Benny Goodman and Glenn Miller. Years later, Jerry recalled the sound of his father playing the clarinet as the family lived at the Amazon Avenue home:

> The clarinet is a wonderful instrument. It has a nice, sonorous quality. I remember the sound of the clarinet more than the tunes. The clarinet had that lovely wood quality, especially in that relaxed middle register. And that sound is very present in my ear. Sounds linger in my ear; I can recall 'em. Some people can recall smells. I can recall specific sounds—I can hear a sound and all of a sudden it will transport me to places.[5]

Jerry's mother also contributed to the music in the Garcia home. Ruth enjoyed music a great deal, but she preferred classical music rather than swing and other popular music of the time. Ruth often played the piano at the Garcia's home.

Both Garcia boys took piano lessons. Jerry studied piano beginning at four or five years of age. However, neither of the boys liked the piano very much, and they were never very good at playing. Jerry was not able to read music particularly well; instead, he preferred to play by ear.[6]

By all accounts, these were idyllic times for the young Garcia family as they balanced work and pleasure. Joe worked hard at the family business, but the Garcias also enjoyed leisure and vacation time together. Once they journeyed nearly 600 miles through the desert by train to visit Las Vegas. More typically, the family toured by car throughout California and the western states, often visiting California's missions, religious outposts established by Spanish settlers between 1769 and 1823 as they attempted to colonize the Pacific region and spread Catholicism to the Native Americans who lived in the area. These travels often brought memorable adventures, including the time when Jerry was a toddler and the family was swimming at a motel pool. A drunken man tossed young Jerry into the pool, and his father had to rescue him. Once his son was safe, Joe proceeded to knock out the drunk.[7]

The family also spent as much time as they could in a cabin they built in Lompico, a wooded area in North Santa Cruz County a few hours south of San Francisco. During the summers, the Garcia and Clifford families spent weeks at a time in Lompico. Sometimes Ruth, the boys, and other family members went to the cabin during the week, and Joe and the other working men in the family joined them on the weekends. The vacations and time at the cabin created many good and long-lasting memories; unfortunately these days were not to last.

DEAR OLD DADDY REST HIS SOUL

The young Garcia family experienced several losses in the mid 1940s. The first trauma occurred when Tiff and Jerry were chopping firewood at the Lompico cabin during the summer of 1946 or the spring of 1947 (the exact date is not known). The boys chopped wood many times and had an established routine: Jerry slid the redwood sticks into place, and Tiff chopped them with an axe. But on one occasion, something went wrong. The two fell out of rhythm, and Tiff cut the middle finger of Jerry's right hand off. Jerry's mother wrapped his hand in a towel as his father rushed them to the nearest hospital. After surgery, Jerry's hand was in several large bandages, and when they finally came off, he was a bit surprised to find that his finger was gone. Yet he soon realized that "it was okay, because as a kid, if you have a few little things that make you different, it's a good score."[8]

While this experience was certainly traumatic for everyone, it was not the biggest tragedy the family experienced. Just days before Jerry was scheduled to begin kindergarten, the Garcias took a trip to the Six Rivers National Forest. Since Tiff was in Lompico with his cousins, Jerry had a unique opportunity to spend the weekend in the outdoors with his father catching fish in the Trinity River. But just one day into the trip, Joe slipped on a rock, and the river's swift current quickly pulled him under the water. Although three fishermen were able to pull Joe from the river, they were not able to resuscitate him. He was under the water at least 10 minutes before they could pull him to the shore. Joe Garcia was pronounced dead at 11:15 p.m., only days after his 45th birthday.

It was a sad twist of fate that this man who had once saved his young son from drowning was not similarly rescued. Jerry later claimed to have witnessed his father being pulled under the water, but Tiff explained that his mother felt it was not possible for Jerry to see his father drown.[9] Newspaper reports of the event do not mention that young Jerry was there, and some believe Jerry heard the account of the tragedy so many times that he believed he saw it happen. Nevertheless, it was a tragedy for both the Garcia and Clifford families, and particularly for young Jerry, who was unable to speak of his father for years to come. As an adult, he captured some of the pain of this experience in haunting drawings.[10]

Life for the Garcia boys changed dramatically after their father's death. Tiff lived for short time with his uncle, a move that required him to change schools. Jerry stayed for a little while with his mother until she sold the family house. Ruth needed money to buy out Joe's partner in the restaurant business, and cash from the sale of her home allowed her to do this. After the house was sold, Ruth moved Jerry and Tiff into her parents' home on Harrington Street, and she moved into a small cottage across the street that her parents owned. Ruth saw the boys mostly on the weekends because she was quite busy during the week trying to keep the restaurant business going. The Garcia family did not particularly approve of her keeping the restaurant and bar; instead, they felt she would do better by returning to nursing. But Ruth was committed to keeping the restaurant and she did so successfully while the boys stayed with her parents. She tried to compensate for not being with the boys by buying things for them, including the first television on their block.

Jerry's grandparents, Bill Clifford and Tillie Olsen, were an odd couple. They had wildly different in personalities, styles, and energy, and Jerry was not sure what might have attracted them to one another.[11] Bill Clifford was a quiet man who provided a solid income and stable home for his family. He worked in the laundry business, primarily as a delivery person. Jerry described his "Pop" as "So Dull [sic] . . . one of the Irish guys that *didn't* have the gift of gab . . . he was just a real studge, you know, he was just yuuuuuh."[12] Bill seemed to love the quiet routines of domestic life, which included caring for Tillie's parrot, Loretta. Tillie found the parrot walking the streets after the San Francisco earthquake, and she became a permanent fixture in the Clifford home. The parrot openly mourned after Bill died.[13]

Jerry's grandmother Tillie was a strong force in Garcia's life. Her father, Captain Olsen, was a Swedish sailor who emigrated to the United States and married a girl of Irish descent. Like the Garcia family, the Olsens shared an interest in music. As a young person, Tillie played the banjo-ukulele, which was popular among women in the 1920s. The banjo-uke has four strings, a neck that is short like the ukulele, and a small banjo body. It has a quieter sound than the banjo, and in the 1920s this was the more typical instrument for women to play. The American banjo originated among African American slaves, and subsequently was taken up by women musicians.[14] Although Tiff Garcia later noted that his grandmother did not play the banjo when he and Jerry were young, her interest in music, along with the Garcia family's musical tendencies, likely had an influence on young Jerry.

Because of Tillie's interests, Jerry learned about country music forms at a young age, including bluegrass founder Bill Monroe's music. Monroe's band was named the Blue Grass Boys after his home state of Kentucky, and over the years the musicians in his band included famous performers like Earl Scruggs, Lester Flatt, Chubby Wise, Howard Watts, Jimmy Martin, Vassar Clements, and others. Bluegrass music is known for its fast tempos, vocal harmonies, and instrumentation, particularly for the mandolin, fiddle, and banjo. This music impressed Jerry, influencing his own performances across his lifetime. Some of his first efforts to pursue a professional career in music involved bluegrass.

Tillie was involved with the laundry business in different ways than her husband. She organized the laundry workers into a union, serving in an elected position as the secretary-treasurer for the organization for a number of years. Tillie spoke at labor conventions and traveled the country. Although Tillie was married, she had extramarital relationships, including one with a man who traveled to labor rallies with her. Bill was well aware of her affairs and did not seem to mind.[15] Jerry described his "Nan" as a handsome woman who loved Hawaii and universal love, and he thought she was outgoing, smart, popular, hardworking, and sassy.[16]

After moving in with their grandparents, Jerry and Tiff attended the Monroe School on Excelsior Boulevard. Jerry did not necessarily like school, but his third grade teacher, Miss Simon, had a profound influence on him. She was instrumental in fostering his early interests in painting and art history. Jerry later described this experience:

> She had everybody in the class . . . making things out of ceramics and paper mache. It was an art thing and that was more or less my guiding interest from that time on. I was going to be a painter and I really was taken with it. I got into art history and all of it. It was finally something for me to do.[17]

Outside of school, Jerry spent a lot of time drawing pictures with his brother Tiff as they worked together to create their own imaginary world. They used laundry pads from his grandparents' house as their canvas.

In addition to art, the two brothers shared other creative interests. They crafted their own musical instruments, including small ukuleles, and they often played the instruments and sang with their cousin Daniel. The boys listened to popular music of the time, including a Bay Area musician called Rusty Draper, along with other well-known artists: Chuck Berry, Buddy Holly, and Eddie Cochran. Tiff later claimed that one of the first 45-rpm records that Jerry bought was a tune Draper recorded called "Gambler's Guitar." Tiff thought this recording, complete with some guitar riffs, may have helped to fuel Jerry's interest in country music.[18]

When they weren't playing music, Tiff and Jerry spent a great deal of time reading comic books. Jerry liked the E.C. comic books, especially the *Tales from the Crypt* horror books. E.C. (Entertaining Comics) was popular in the 1940s and 1950s, publishing a range of comic books that focused on horror, science fiction, and fantasy. Beginning in 1948, however, the industry came under public scrutiny from critics like Frederic Wertham, who argued in his book *Seduction of the Innocent* (1954) that such books were harmful to children. William Gaines, the editor for E.C., was called to testify before a U.S. Senate subcommittee that scrutinized his work. Shortly after this, public backlash from the accusations against E.C. and the approval of a Comics Code that regulated the content of comic books caused William Gaines to focus his business exclusively on producing MAD magazine, a satirical comic book that poked fun at all aspects of American life. The influences of E.C. and MAD are evident in Jerry's childhood art as well as some of the work he created later in life.[19]

Outside of their home, the Garcia boys found entertainment in a variety of places. When they had some money in hand, they went to the movie theater. One of Jerry's favorite movies was the 1948 horror-comedy film *Abbot and Costello Meet Frankenstein*. If they had no money for the theater, they went to the beach or the zoo, or they frequented the parks and playgrounds in their neighborhood. Sometimes the boys found mischief, breaking windows or setting small fires. Once they broke 60 windows in the back of a building. For some reason, they did not notice that the building was a police station. When the police officers found the boys, they took them home.[20] Another time, the brothers put a small firework called a cherry bomb in a barber's red and white glass pole. Needless to say, the glass exploded everywhere and the boys were again in a bit of trouble.

Jerry had asthma as a child, and he could never run very far without wheezing. When his asthma flared up, Jerry needed to have a shot of epinephrine. After a bout with asthma, he usually rested in bed for a few days to recover, reading books and comics, and listening to music. While Jerry would later tell others that he experienced a sickly childhood, his brother Tiff disagreed. Tiff remembered that the bouts with asthmas were infrequent and that Jerry was pampered with gifts when they did occur.[21]

In the late 1940s, Ruth had to move her hotel and bar to a new location across the street because the Sailor's Union of the Pacific bought her property to construct a meeting hall. When she moved the business into its new space, Jerry and Tiff helped to clean the rooms in the hotel, and they spent time interacting with the sailors who frequented the bar. Jerry found it quite entertaining to hang out at the bar, listening to stories the sailors told of their travels to the Persian Gulf and the Far East. He later recalled:

> I grew up in a bar. . . . And that was back in the days when the Orient was still the Orient, and it hadn't been completely Americanized yet. They'd bring back all these weird things. Like one guy had the largest private collection of photographs of square-riggers. He was an old sea captain, and he had a mint condition '47 Packard that he parked out front. And he had a huge wardrobe of these beautifully tailored double-breasted suits from the '30s. And he'd tell these incredible stories. That was one of the reasons I couldn't stay in school [later]. School was a little too boring. These guys gave me a glimpse into a larger universe that seemed attractive and fun and, you know, crazy.[22]

In spite of hanging around his mother's business, however, Jerry did not get to see much of his mother or spend much time with her. She worked a great deal trying to keep the bar and hotel operating, and she did maintain a bit of a social life. When the Sailor's Union construction project was underway, Ruth met a carpenter named Ben Brown who was working on the new building. The two were married in 1949, but the marriage was short-lived.

Ruth wed for a third time in 1953 to Wally Matusiewicz, a merchant seaman. When Wally married Ruth, he took over the majority of her business operations so that she could spend more time with her sons. Jerry never cared for Wally. He reportedly had a temper and was hard on young Jerry. When he could, 11-year-old Jerry escaped to his grandmother Tillie's house.[23]

Shortly after Ruth married Wally, the Union Oil Company decided to move its office to the space where her bar was located, so once again Ruth needed to move her business. This time she found space across the street from the former 400 Club in San Francisco. Tiff later reported that his mother operated the biggest day business of any bar in the city, with people frequenting the bar at all hours and renting rooms in the upstairs for months on end.[24] Ruth's business seemed to be successful in many ways, and with the marriage to Wally, she finally seemed able to return to the more traditional life she yearned for as a housewife with her sons in her home.

LET MY INSPIRATION FLOW

As the bar business boomed, Ruth and Wally decided to move to Menlo Park in San Mateo County, a suburb about 30 miles south of the city. They had a new house on a cul-de-sac, and a new beige Cadillac in the driveway. The move was a big change for Tiff and Jerry, who was about 11 years old at the time. Everything was new to them, and while that could bring a good deal of excitement and fun, it could also be quite difficult. The boys were separated from their grandparents for the first time in their lives and were only able to visit with them on the weekends. Jerry and Tiff both needed to make new friends and establish new relationships.

Jerry attended the Menlo-Oaks Middle School, but he did not like it very much, nor was he a star pupil. He generally found school to be boring. Years later, however, Jerry credited the teachers at Menlo-Oaks for opening up the world to him and for engaging his questions. Dwight Johnson, a seventh-grade teacher, sparked Jerry's interest in a variety of books and encouraged him to think deeply. Jerry had always been a reader, but Mr. Johnson pushed him beyond science fiction, comics, and the typical books that Jerry picked up on his own.[25] Mr. Johnson and a few other teachers recognized that Jerry was bright, and they helped to enroll Jerry in a school program at Stanford University so that he would be challenged in his academic work. Jerry read George Orwell's book *1984*, a variety of philosophy, and anything else he could get his hands on, a habit that would continue through his adult life. Books opened a new world for Jerry, one that was different than school.

At Menlo-Oaks, Jerry hung out with a group of roughneck boys who often bullied other kids they encountered. One day they hazed Laird Grant, and in spite of their unlikely introduction, Jerry and Laird soon became lifelong friends. Laird spent time at Jerry's house, and the boys frequently roamed the streets together. Sometimes late at night they broke into the Golden State Dairy, across the street from Jerry's house, in search of chocolate milk and ice cream.[26]

The Garcia family did not reside in Menlo Park for long. After approximately two years, they moved back to the city, eventually settling into the large apartment over the family business at the 400 Club. Soon Tiff graduated from high school and joined the Marines, which brought another dramatic change for Jerry. Tiff was stationed at Camp Pendelton in San Diego, and Jerry would not see him very often after this. Up to this point in his life, Jerry always had Tiff, while other people, like his mother and grandparents, were in and out of his life for various reasons. Now the two would find themselves going separate ways.

Once he was back in the city, Jerry attended James Denman Middle School, where there were stark social class divisions among the student body. Jerry's school had two distinct groups: the Barts (short for Black Barts or Greasers), which included the kids from working-class families, and the Shoes (short for White Shoe, clean cut students in the style of then-popular singer Pat Boone), the students from the middle-class and more well-to-do families. The gangs always fought with one another, in school and in the neighborhoods, and Jerry, who was a Bart, was injured a few times as a result.

These social troubles continued even when Jerry went to Balboa High School in the 10th grade. Jerry knew this was a rough school, and he understood that he had to be a hoodlum in order to survive. Yet Jerry's cousin Daniel never remembered Jerry getting into fights.[27] He never saw Jerry as a tough guy; instead, Jerry remained an avid reader, and the two cousins shared a growing fascination with new music that was causing quite a sensation at the time: rock and roll.

Some of Jerry's early interest in rock music grew from watching movies. When Jerry was in the city on the weekends, he often went to the movies with his cousin Daniel. One particularly memorable movie sparked his imagination. *Rock around the Clock* (1956), which featured Bill Haley and His Comets, relayed a fictionalized version of how rock and roll began. Although the storyline was thin, moviegoers did not seem to mind. They were more interested in the music, which included Alan Freed, The Platters (who performed the song "The Great Pretender"), and Freddie Bell and the Bell Boys. Although it was a major box office success, the film was banned in some parts of the world because of violence in the theaters where it was shown.

Jerry's musical interests up to this point had largely been influenced by Tiff. Tiff listened to R&B radio stations in San Francisco in the 1950s, and he shared that interest with Jerry. Before he joined the military, Tiff often took Jerry to record shops to buy records by Bill Haley and other musicians popular at the time. Jerry regularly listened to Chuck Berry, Buddy Holly, and Eddie Cochran. He also liked Bo Diddley, James Burton, and Chicago blues musicians.

Jerry sang popular tunes of the day with his cousin Daniel, and he wanted more than anything to have a guitar. Seemingly oblivious to Jerry's wishes, Ruth gave him an accordion for his 15th birthday. Of course Jerry was not too excited about this, and he begged his mother to let him trade the accordion for a guitar he saw in a local pawnshop. Eventually she agreed, and Jerry became the proud owner of his first electric guitar, a used Danelectro. There was enough money left on the trade to purchase a small amp. Jerry had no idea how to play, and he did not have anyone who could teach him, so he worked on learning the instrument on his own with the help of a few books. Jerry studied pictures of guitar players to see how they held the instrument and how their hands were positioned to played chords. He was determined to learn. In time, Jerry and his cousin Daniel played well enough to perform at various family functions, and the two wrote a few simple songs together.

After his 15th birthday, Jerry spent most of his time playing guitar and hanging out with his friends, and he became more and more interested in visual arts. In 1958, Jerry took art classes at the California School of Fine Arts, now known as the San Francisco Art Institute. He was part of a special program for high school students who showed some talent in the arts. Jerry studied first with Wally Hedrick, a beat generation artist who was one of the founders of the Gallery Six where writers like Jack Kerouac, Neal Cassady and Allen Ginsberg, who read his famous poem *Howl* publicly for this first time in this venue, congregated. Hedrick was an early pioneer of American pop art and funk art, and he also did a lot of work in metal. Hedrick helped Jerry with his painting, recognizing that the boy seemed to be drawn to what later became known as the California figurative style, known for its sensual brushwork yet recognizable imagery.[28] Hedrick was a strong influence on Garcia. He introduced Jerry to the Beatnik culture by encouraging him to attend poetry readings at local cafes, read Jack Kerouac's book *On the Road*, and listen to acoustic blues guitar music.[29] Kerouac's work would have a lasting influence on Garcia, and Kerouac's photo later hung in his dressing room.[30]

Jerry also took art lessons with Elmer Bischoff, an abstract artist among the first generation of Bay Area figurative painters. Bischoff was known for putting feeling in his work. Bischoff encouraged Jerry to use oil paint and try a more abstract style. It was likely the only time that Jerry experimented with oil in his artwork; instead, he preferred watercolors, acrylics, and other mediums.

In spite of his connections with the California School of Fine Arts and his interests in music, Jerry's mother remained concerned about him. He spent a lot of time on the streets, and she was not sure the city was the best place for him. She knew that Jerry was smoking pot and experimenting with pills. To get him out of the city, Ruth decided to move the family north of San Francisco to Cazadero, a Sonoma County community situated in the midst of redwood trees. Here, Jerry was scheduled to attend Analy High School; however, Ruth's plans never materialized. Jerry skipped school, taking his mother's car to visit a girlfriend in Redwood City, and he finally decided that he would drop out of high school. In January 1960, Jerry was not sure what he might do with his life. Things were not going well with his family, and he needed to get away. He made a dramatic decision, the only alternative he could think of at the time: Jerry joined the army.

NOTES

1. Blair Jackson, *Garcia: An American Life*. New York: The Penguin Group, 1999.

2. Ibid.

3. Ibid., p. 6.

4. Ibid.

5. Ibid., p. 8.

6. Holly George-Warren, *Garcia: By the Editors of The Rolling Stone*. New York: Little Brown and Company, 1995.

7. Jerry Garcia, *Harrington Street*. New York: Delacourt Press, 1995.

8. Jackson, 1999, p. 9.

9. Ibid.

10. Garcia, 1995.

11. Ibid.

12. Ibid., n.p.

13. Ibid.

14. For a history of the banjo in the United States, see Philip Gura and James Bollman, *America's Instrument: The Banjo in the Nineteenth Century*. Chapel Hill: University of North Carolina Press, 1999.

15. Jackson, 1999.

16. Garcia, 1995.

17. April Higashi, *Jerry Garcia: The Collected Artwork*. New York: Thunders Mouth Press, 2005, p. xviii.

18. Jackson, 1999.

19. See Higashi, 2005, for examples of these influences.

20. Robert Greenfield, *Dark Star*. New York: William Morrow and Company, 1996.

21. Jackson, 1999.

22. Blair Jackson, http://www.blairjackson.com/chapter_one_additions.htm (accessed November 23, 2008).

23. Greenfield, 1996.

24. Jackson, 1999.

25. Ibid.

26. Ibid.

27. Ibid.

28. Ibid.

29. Dennis McNally, *A Long Strange Trip*. New York: Broadway Books, 2002.

30. Gary Ciocco, "How Dead Beats Became Deadheads: From Emerson and James to Kerouac and Garcia." In S. Gimbel (Ed.), *The Grateful Dead and Philosophy*, pp. 63–74. Peru, IL: Open Court Publishing, 2007.

Chapter 2

CATS UNDER THE STARS

I wonder who they are, the men who really run this land, and I wonder why they run it with such a thoughtless hand . . . peace is not an
awful lot to ask.

—*"What Are Their Names,"* If Only I Could Remember My Name,
Young, Garcia, Lesh, Schrieve, and Crosby (1971)

Jerry Garcia completed basic training at Fort Ord, California, about 125
miles south of San Francisco. Between April and July of 1960, he earned
honors for carbine sharpshooting and basic missileman training. When
basic training was finished, Garcia attended service school to learn to be
an auto maintenance helper, and then he went to his initial base assignment at Fort Winfield Scott in San Francisco.

When Jerry enlisted in the military, the United States had been involved with the Vietnam conflict for a number of years. President Dwight
D. Eisenhower deployed the Military Assistance Advisory Group to Vietnam in November of 1955 to train the South Vietnamese army. Although
American troop buildup in Vietnam would not intensify until 1965, the
conflict must certainly have been in the minds of the officers and soldiers
at Forts Ord and Winfield Scott.

Jerry Garcia was not well suited for the army, and he was really out of
place at Fort Winfield Scott. Jerry explained:

It's absolutely the top of the elite. . . . It's the nicest place to be
stationed; all the guys who are there have jockeyed and manipulated to get in there. They don't want no trouble, you know

what I mean? Every single guy there is a guy who's got gold-plated service . . . so there I was going AWOL on weekends and screwing up left and right, and just doing my stuff. I wasn't committing crimes or anything like that. I was just living my life. And even doing things that I thought were important.[1]

Throughout basic training, school, and his initial assignment, Jerry continued to hang out with his girlfriend in Redwood City and with Laird Grant, his childhood friend, and he spent as much time as he could playing his guitar, a Sears Silvertone. Jerry was often late to roll call and absent without leave (AWOL) from the base. Since the army does not tolerate this kind of behavior, Jerry ended up in front of a military court. The details of his conviction are not particularly clear, but one fact is evident: Jerry Garcia was discharged from the army after nine months of service. He was free to explore the civilian world and find his way.

LOVERS WE GOT TO BE, LOVERS WE ARE

After his brief stint in the military, Garcia headed to Palo Alto, California, where he hung out in several bookstores and cafes. Palo Alto is home to Stanford University, and as a university town, the community had many progressive people, artists, and activists for Jerry to befriend. One of his favorite places was Kepler's Bookstore, founded in 1955 by Roy Kepler, a conscientious objector during World War II and a noted peace advocate. Jerry frequented the store with a guitar in hand, writing poetry and music almost daily. He found a place to live at the Chateau, a large house with rooms for rent in Menlo Park, just a mile from Kepler's. Many artists, musicians, and poets, including Robert Hunter, lived at the Chateau. A skilled conversationalist, Garcia enjoyed long talks with friends and acquaintances about philosophy and other things that were on his mind. Jerry was known to be cool and funny, but not necessarily friendly.

Garcia's conversations likely touched on local, national, and world events of the time. In the early 1960s, residents of the Palo Alto region enjoyed a comfortable economy, fueled in part by aerospace and military industries like the Lockheed Martin plant, the Stanford Research Institute, and the Watkins-Johnson Company. The nation as a whole was hopeful in spite of building tensions and rising concerns about Vietnam and the ongoing Cold War. The Russians had launched Sputnik in 1957, and the space race was underway as Americans attempted to put the first man on the moon. Space travel fascinated Garcia, fueled in part by his vivid imagination and love for science fiction. When John F. Kennedy was inaugurated as the 35th President of the United States, the nation looked to him for leadership that would overcome international concerns and problematic social and domestic issues in the country. Rachel Carson's book *Silent Spring* (1962) brought attention to environmental concerns, Betty Friedan's book *The Feminine Mystique* (1963) contributed to the growing women's rights movement, and Martin Luther King Jr. attempted to bring peaceful resolution to the civil rights unrest that characterized much of the 1950s and 1960s.

As he moved in and out of the coffee houses in Palo Alto, Jerry began to keep company with Robert Hunter, and soon the two began collaborating in songwriting, a partnership that lasted a lifetime. Alan Trist hung out with Jerry at Kepler's, and he later became part of the management team for the Grateful Dead. Jerry also spent a good deal of time talking with Willy Legate, impressed with his deep understandings of Marxist theory.[2] Barbara Meier, who was 15 years of age, was also a regular in Jerry's circle. She first met Jerry when her friend Sue invited him to join them on a hike. The two girls met Jerry at the Skylight Art Supply store, and when Jerry looked in the car and saw Barbara, he asked Sue to tell her that he loved her.[3] The three went on a hike, and Jerry sang Joan Baez songs on the way home in the car. Barbara was soon seduced by Jerry, and she enjoyed hanging out with him and his friends Robert Hunter and Alan Trist as they wrote music and poems. Barbara, who was quite beautiful, worked as a fashion model. Her image appeared in local and national magazine advertisements. Barbara often used the money from her modeling gigs to buy cigarettes and other necessities for Jerry, and she also bought him his first acoustic guitar.[4] Jerry was helpful to Barbara as well, encouraging her to go to art school. Jerry later described her as "the love of my life, really, in a way."[5]

Jerry often went to parties where he formed other friendships and acquaintances. One memorable friendship was with Paul Speegle, a 16-year-old high school student who was the son of a *San Francisco Call-Bulletin* drama and music critic. Paul was an artist and quite involved with local theater groups when he met Jerry, and the two seemed to hit it off quite well. Through his friendship with Paul, Jerry briefly became involved with the Commedia Theater. Yet this friendship was unfortunately short-lived. In the early morning hours of February 20, 1961, Paul was hanging out at a party with Jerry and Alan Trist, and as the party was winding down, the three loaded into Lee Adams's car. Adams, who had too much to drink, drove too fast and failed to negotiate a turn. As they crashed, Jerry was thrown out of the car, and the impact caused him to suffer a shoulder injury and lose his shoes. Alan's back was hurt, and Lee ended up with a mild head injury. Young Paul Speegle, however, was killed instantly. Jerry later explained that the crash was "where my life began. Before then I was always living at less than capacity. I was idling. That was the slingshot for the rest of my life."[6]

The changes in Jerry's life were not immediately apparent after the car accident. Jerry continued to play guitar in small public venues like St. Michael's Alley in Palo Alto, widening his experiences with music and public performance. By this time, he traded his Sears guitar for an acoustic one, and Barbara bought him a Stella 12-string. One of his early groups included David Nelson and Bob Hunter (bass, guitar, and banjo). The musicians were largely self-taught, slowing records down or playing the same track over and over again to learn new tunes. It was a fun and lively time for Garcia and his friends as they jammed together and explored music. Garcia began to play banjo in earnest, and he delved more seriously into bluegrass music and old-time music, including music by the Carter family. His passion for this genre would remain throughout his life.

In the early 1960s, folk music, or the people's music, grew in popularity in urban areas across the United States. Palo Alto was home to The Kingston Trio, formed in 1957, which set an early although somewhat polished standard for folk music. Some notable artists who were part of this movement included Woodie Guthrie, Pete Seeger, native Palo Altoan Joan Baez, Judy Collins, and Bob Dylan. These famous musicians, along with less well-known local talents, contributed to political and social discourse through their combinations of folk and pop music. Folks artists performed in the coffee houses, bookstores, and festivals, and the music became a critical aspect of the early counterculture movement that characterized the 1960s.

Although Jerry was not particularly enamored with the political aspects of folk music, he certainly engaged the genre, eventually forming a group called the Thunder Mountain Tub Thumpers. The group played well enough to open for the Stanford University Folk Festival on May 11, 1962. Joe Edminston played banjo, Ken Frankel played fiddle, Robert Hunter played mandolin, and Jerry played guitar. This was one of several short-lived bands that Jerry organized or was a member of during the early 1960s.

Although the Tub Thumpers did not perform as a group for very long, Jerry and his friend Robert Hunter continued to practice together, joining with David Nelson. The trio frequented the Boar's Head, where they played alongside other young and hopeful artists. These experiences expanded their repertoire and skills, and eventually the membership of their group. At this venue, Jerry became acquainted with Ron McKernan (a.k.a. Pigpen), who played piano, harmonica, and acoustic guitar. Soon enough,

Pigpen and Garcia became close friends, sharing a love for the blues, and in no time the two were playing music together on a regular basis.

McKernan's deep appreciation for the blues was due in part to his father's influence. McKernan's father worked as a rhythm and blues disc jockey in the 1950s, and Pigpen became a student of African American influences on the blues. In addition to his vast knowledge of the music form, Pigpen also knew about the artists' personal lives and much of the lore that surrounded this music. Pigpen was able to teach Jerry a great deal about the blues. Pigpen's physical appearance was a bit unusual and off-putting to some, but this was not the kind of thing that would bother Jerry Garcia. Their friendship was intense, due in part to their shared respect for one another and their love for music.

Phil Lesh, who later became the bass player for the Grateful Dead, joined Jerry's scene in 1962. The two connected at a party and they frequently hung out together at Kepler's Bookstore, St. Michaels, and the Peace Center. Lesh thought Garcia looked like the late composer Claude Debussy,[7] and he liked Garcia's music and style. Lesh had more formal and schooled experiences with music than Jerry did. He played violin and trumpet as a child, and he studied music composition, with particular interests in avant-garde classical music (Charles Ives, George Gershwin, Claude Debussy, and others) as well as free jazz (Cecil Taylor, John Coltrane, Sun Ra). Lesh also studied music at Mills College in Oakland.

After hearing Jerry sing an old border ballad called "Maddy Groves," Lesh decided to make a demo of Jerry's performance to play for Gert Chiarito, a producer at KPFA, a radio station where Lesh worked. Lesh was impressed with the way in which Jerry delivered the song with simplicity and directness. KPFA was the first public radio station in the country, and Roy Kepler helped to develop it. The demo led to Garcia doing an entire show for *The Midnight Special*, the folk show at KPFA. Garcia, who was just 19 years of age at the time, deeply impressed Chiarito, especially when he played "Long Black Veil."[8]

To help make ends meet, Jerry taught music lessons at Dana Morgan's music store in Palo Alto. He tried to help his students to hear the music. Jerry wanted his students to listen to the songs they wished to play on recordings and then learn to play the guitar part. But Jerry was not a particularly patient teacher. Once Jerry became so discouraged when a student was not progressing as expected that he excused himself from the lesson to use the restroom and never returned.[9] Despite the challenges the students presented, teaching music allowed Jerry to continue to play guitar and practice music all day. He was not interested in doing much else, and he did not seem to mind that he had little money and few possessions. All that mattered were his guitar and cigarettes.

A few of the musicians who hung around Dana's store played with Jerry, including Bill Kreutzmann, a percussionist who later became a member of the Grateful Dead, and a 15-year-old named Bob Weir. Weir wanted to improve his guitar playing, and he liked to hear Jerry play, but the two were not fast friends. Weir was five years younger than Jerry, and he came from an affluent family. Garcia was a well-read, self-taught intellectual, whereas Weir was dyslexic and athletic.[10] Garcia was unkempt with long curly hair, while Weir appeared to be clean-cut and was generally considered to be good looking. Yet in spite of their differences, the two did share some commonalities: both did not fit into the 1950s-influenced social scene in high school, and both loved to play guitar. Weir hung around the Palo Alto scene, listening to music by artists like Jorma Kaukonen, a founding member of the psychedelic band Jefferson Airplane, someone Jerry deeply respected as a musician. But the similarities between Garcia and Weir soon surpassed their differences, and the two became life-long band mates, performing side by side in countless concerts and venues.

AIN'T IT CRAZY

In 1962, Jerry's close friend Robert Hunter participated in the Menlo Park Veteran Administration's program testing the effects of psychedelic drugs on people. Hunter earned $140 for participating in four research sessions at Stanford, one per week for four weeks. During the sessions, he was administered psychedelic drugs, including mescaline, psilocybin, and lysergic acid diethylamide (LSD). The testing was part of the Central Intelligence Agency's (CIA) efforts to find a speech-inducing or "truth" drug to use on prisoners of war. This effort began under the auspices of the Office of Strategic Services (OSS) in the 1940s with tests on highly potent forms of marijuana and, after World War II, continued under the newly created CIA with tests on heroin and LSD.[11] Hunter was enthralled by the experience, and once he explained it to his good friend, Jerry was convinced he needed to experience the same thing. At the time, psychedelics were not illegal; instead, they were considered to be a way to expand human understandings of the mind and subconscious. The fact that they might be dangerous, cause harm, or result in long-term addictions or health problems was not evident.

Jerry took LSD for the first time with David Nelson and Sara Ruppenthal in 1965. Sara Ruppenthal read Aldous Huxley's book *Doors of Perception* (1954), which instigated her interest in and fascination with psychedelics. Huxley took mescaline, a psychedelic drug, and then wrote about his experience, arguing that these drugs were a way to open a person's mind. Huxley's text and his personal experimentation with LSD set the stage for much interest in mescaline, and his words reflected the views of many people who experimented with these drugs: "We live together, we act on, and react to, one another; but always and in all circumstances we are by ourselves."[12] Shortly after his relationship with Barbara Meier ended, Jerry met Sara Ruppenthal as he was walking across the Stanford Shopping Center parking lot, guitar in hand. Jerry hitched a ride on her bicycle, and the two quickly hit it off.[13] As a Stanford University student, Sara was active in the peace movement and was into folk music. She enjoyed listening to Garcia, Nelson, and Hunter playing in the back room of Kepler's bookstore. A relationship quickly developed between Sara and Jerry as they began to share their love for music and one another. The couple made a few public appearances together with Sara singing and playing the autoharp or guitar.

Jerry and Sara enjoyed a passionate, carefree time together, but their happy-go-lucky days were short-lived. Just a few weeks into their relationship as they were window-shopping, Sara told Jerry she was pregnant with his child. Sara was quite scared and not sure what to do. Her relationship with Jerry had already brought her considerable trouble, particularly when she was kicked out of college after being caught staying with Jerry overnight. Dormitories had strict rules, and universities had social honor codes students were required to abide by, and Sara's behavior violated these. Sara knew Jerry wanted to be a professional musician, and neither of them had adequate means to support themselves, let alone a baby. But none of this seemed of particular concern to Jerry. When Sara told him about the baby, he replied, "Well, I've always wanted to get married. Let's get hitched."[14] In spite of strong objections from Sara's family and Jerry's friends, Jerry and Sara married at the Palo Alto Unitarian Church on April 23, 1963. The couple's daughter, Heather, was born December 8, 1963.

Shortly after Sara and Jerry married, they traded in some of their musical instruments and, combined with money they received as wedding gifts, purchased a Weyman banjo from the 1930s. Jerry began to practice long hours, hoping to be skilled enough to support his family with the money he earned from gigs. He seemed to have potential. Less than a month after they were married, Jerry performed at the Monterey County Fairgrounds, winning an amateur bluegrass competition for his performance with the Wildwood Boys. At the same festival, he had the chance to listen to some popular performers, including the folk trio Peter, Paul, and Mary, Joan Baez, and Bob Dylan.

Although Jerry's banjo playing did not necessarily meet the high standards for perfection that is typical in bluegrass music, he continued to pursue a career as a bluegrass musician, and in early 1964, his band mates in the Black Mountain Boys group, Sandy Rothman and David Nelson, decided to travel east with Garcia hoping to find work with Bill Monroe, the Father of Bluegrass. Monroe's band, The Bluegrass Boys, was quite popular in the 1960s, and earning a spot with Monroe's band would have been a dream come true for the young musicians; however, they had no well-formulated plan, and when the group finally had the opportunity to see Monroe, they never asked him for a job.

Shortly after seeing Monroe, Jerry returned to California to see Sara and baby Heather. While he may have been disappointed in the outcome of this adventure, his future was about to take a dramatic change for the better. Soon he would be playing with a group that would change his life forever.

HERE COMES SUNSHINE

When he realized that a bluegrass band was not going to work out for him, Jerry decided to put together a jug band. This kind of musical group did not require particularly skilled musicians, and the form was freer than the bluegrass music Jerry had been trying to play. Jug bands were known for having traditional instruments, like guitars and mandolins, along with homemade instruments, including a jug, a washboard, spoons, and other combinations. The bands played folk and old-time music, and the musicians were not held to the same tight technique standards that bluegrass players were. This freed Jerry to be more imaginative in his playing. His friends Bob Weir, Pigpen, and Bob Matthews joined Jerry's group, originally called Mother McCree's Uptown Jug Champions. The ensemble played at Top of the Tangent, a folk club on the top floor of the Tangent Pizza Parlor popular with Stanford students. Jerry often ran into other up-and-coming musicians in these scenes, including Janis Joplin and Jorma Kaukonen, who made their rounds at the Tangent and other local venues where Jerry played.

Unfortunately, although Mother McCree's was willing to play anywhere they could, jug bands were not getting a lot of gigs in those days. As a result, Mother McCree's started to experiment with electric sounds, leaning toward blues music because of Pigpen's interests, but clearly evolving into a rock band.[15] They changed their name to the Warlocks, in part because of Weir's interest in *Lord of the Rings*, and more of Jerry's friends joined the group: Pigpen played organ, Bill Kreutzmann played percussion, and Dana

Morgan played bass. The Warlocks were in a fortunate position: they did not need too much money for instruments because they could borrow what they needed from Morgan's music store.

The Warlocks' first official gig was at Magoo's Pizza Parlor in Menlo Park in May 1965, where some local high school students showed up to hear them play. Word spread that the group was pretty good, and by their third gig, hundreds of people attended. The Warlocks played music made popular by other well-known bands at the time, including the Rolling Stones, the Kinks, and old Chuck Berry tunes. Jerry's friend Phil Lesh went to hear the band at Magoo's, dancing to the music even though it was not permitted in the parlor, and his life changed forever.[16] Jerry knew Lesh was talented and just beginning to learn to play the bass guitar, and he also knew that Lesh had perfect pitch. Jerry had become increasingly annoyed with Dana Morgan because he was not particularly good at playing bass, and he was an obvious weak spot in the band. Jerry was concerned that Morgan would prevent them from getting more gigs, so he decided to ask Phil to take Dana's place and become a regular with the band. It was a risk because Phil was new to the instrument, but he agreed to give it a try. Unfortunately this meant they would need to come up with some money for the band's equipment since Morgan would no longer let them borrow freely from his store.

Many musicians influenced Garcia's understanding of music as he performed with the Warlocks, including The Beatles. Garcia once noted:

> [The Beatles] were real important to everybody. They were a little model, especially the movies—the movies were a big turn-on. Just because it was a little model of good times. The Fifties were sure hurting for good times. And the early Sixties were very serious too—Kennedy and everything. And the Beatles were light and having a good time and they were good too, so it was a combination that was very satisfying on the artistic level, which is part of the scene that I was into—the art school thing and all that.[17]

Garcia later claimed that blues guitarist Freddie King had the greatest influence on him as a guitar player, particularly when he started to play electric with the Warlocks. Jerry listened closely to the phrasing on his albums, including *Here's Freddie King*.[18]

Soon enough the new band would generate a great deal of attention through regular performances at Ken Kesey's parties. Kesey, who became famous when he authored the book *One Flew Over the Cuckoo's Nest*

(1962) based on his personal experiences with government-sponsored drug testing, frequently hosted bashes at his home in La Honda, California, near Palo Alto. The parties included an eclectic group of people who called themselves the Merry Band of Pranksters. Owsley "Bear" Stanley, who earned a reputation for making LSD, was among the group, as was the poet Allen Ginsberg and the infamous Neal Cassady (the inspiration for the character Dean Moriarty in Kerouac's *On the Road* [1957] and a central figure in the beatnik movement of the 1950s). The Pranksters shared many adventures, including a trip in a painted school bus dubbed "Further" across the country to New York and the World's Fair during the summer of 1964. The Pranksters and others who attended Kesey's parties took acid regularly, and some lived communally at Kesey's home.

Many young people attending Kesey's parties, including Jerry Garcia, were influenced by Jack Kerouac's book *On the Road*. The beatnik message of the book appealed to these young people who grew up in the 1950s and joined the counterculture in the 1960s, and it was exciting for them to be around icons of the era like Neal Cassady. Cassady was known to be an amazing storyteller, an intellectual, and a wild driver. Cassady had a tremendous influence on Garcia, helping him to understand how as an artist you could "*be* the work," solidifying Garcia's commitment to being part of a dynamic group.[19] Garcia later explained of Cassady:

> He was the first person I met who he himself was the art. He was an artist and he was the art also. He was doing it consciously, as well. He worked with the world . . . he was that guy in the real world. He scared a lot of people. A lot of people thought he was crazy. . . . Most people I know didn't understand him at all. . . . He liked musicians; he always liked to hang out with musicians. That's why he sort of picked up on us.[20]

When they performed for the Acid Tests, parties where guests experimented openly and freely with psychedelic drugs, the Warlocks played an eclectic mix of music, including many tunes that they played in the jug band. They were certainly different than other bands at that time, often playing with a sense of reckless abandon. At the Acid Tests the band could experiment freely in a setting that really made no demands on them, and they soon came to realize that "art could be lived."[21] The Acid Tests gave them experience that they could not have in any other context. They could improvise and try new things, and those who were listening were very accepting.

In time the Acid Tests were held throughout the Palo Alto area and in cities that included Portland and Los Angeles. The parties were not advertised, with the exception of fliers Kesey and the Pranksters made that presented his challenge: "Can you pass the acid test?" As word spread about the parties, the crowds and enthusiasm grew, eventually filling venues as large as the Longshoreman's Hall in San Francisco. Since acid was not illegal at the time, the authorities were not able to stop the events, as alarming as they may have been.

One Prankster was Carolyn Adams, who Neal Cassady renamed "Mountain Girl." Soon after joining the acid tests, she became involved in a relationship with Ken Kesey and discovered she was expecting her first child. But there were troubles ahead for the two. Kesey was arrested for marijuana possession and ordered to six months in the county jail and probation terms that included severing all ties with the Pranksters. Although Kesey planned to appeal the sentence, he was caught just a few nights after his arrest with more pot and in Mountain Girl's company.[22] Kesey knew he faced a much more serious penalty now, probably an extended time in jail, and so he took Mountain Girl on the lam to Mexico. Their daughter, Sunshine, was born there in May 1966. To ensure the baby would hold U.S. citizenship, Mountain Girl married another Prankster named George Walker because she could not marry Kesey. He was still married to his wife, Faye.

Another regular at the Acid Tests was Jerry's wife Sara. She frequently took baby Heather along with her, leaving the child in a safe place with crayons and toys, or in a sleeping bag while she enjoyed the party. But in this context, Jerry and Sara soon realized they had little in common beyond acid and Heather, and they understood their marriage was not going to last. Jerry later explained that one of the effects of his experimentation with acid was, "It freed me, because I suddenly realized that my little attempt at having a straight life and doing that was really a fiction and just wasn't going to work out."[23] When Sara suspected that Jerry was with another woman, she left him for a Prankster. Times were changing, and so were the Warlocks.

NOTES

1. Blair Jackson, http://www.blairjackson.com/chapter_one_additions.htm (accessed November 23, 2008).

2. Blair Jackson, *Garcia: An American Life*. New York: The Penguin Group, 1999.

3. Robert Greenfield, *Dark Star*. New York: William Morrow and Company, 1996.

4. Ibid.

5. Dennis McNally, *A Long Strange Trip*. New York: Broadway Books, 2002, p. 37.

6. Jackson, 1999, p. 33.

7. Phil Lesh, *Searching for the Sound*. New York: Little Brown and Company, 2005.

8. McNally, 2002.

9. Lesh, 2005.

10. McNally, 2002.

11. For a history of drug testing, see Martin Lee and Bruce Shlain, *Acid Dreams: The Complete Social History of LSD: The CIA, the Sixties and Beyond*. New York: Grove Press, 1985.

12. Aldous Huxley, *The Doors of Perception*. New York: Harper & Bros., 1954, p. 12.

13. Lesh, 2005.

14. Jackson, 1999, p. 55.

15. Holly George-Warren, *Garcia: By the Editors of The Rolling Stone*. New York: Little Brown and Company, 1995.

16. Lesh, 2005.

17. Jerry Garcia, Charles Reich, and Jann Wenner, *Garcia: A Signpost to a New Space*. New York: De Capo Press, 1972, p. 14.

18. George-Warren, 1995.

19. Paul Gass, "Buddhism through the Eyes of the Dead," in Steven Gimbel (Ed.), *The Grateful Dead and Philosophy*. Peru, IL: Open Court Publishing, pp. 127–37, 2007, p. 128.

20. Jackson, 1999, p. 93.

21. Horace Fairlamb, "Community at the Edge of Chaos: The Dead's Cultural Revolution," in Steven Gimbel (Ed.), *The Grateful Dead and Philosophy*. Peru, IL: Open Court Publishing, pp. 13–26, 2007.

22. Jackson, 1999.

23. Ibid., p. 98.

Chapter 3

COMES A TIME

Our audience is like people who like licorice. Not everybody likes
licorice, but the people who like licorice really like licorice.

—*Jerry Garcia, December 10, 1981,*
to Geraldo Rivera on NBC's 20/20 news magazine

As they played the Acid Tests and other local venues in the early 1960s,
the Warlocks began to find their sound and grow in popularity. The band
members became a unit, even with the individual directions and unique
contributions from each person. Garcia described being a member of the
Warlocks as both commitment and liberation.[1] The group played louder
and longer, one night after another, rejecting the conventions of the folk
music world and instead embracing performances that were spontaneous
and different. Inspired in part by John Coltrane, the jazz saxophonist,
Garcia and Lesh led their band mates into the improvisational world,
which became one of the most distinguishing features of their live performances in the years to come. The two also grew to respect each other
as musicians. Garcia explained that Lesh was not like other bass players:
"He doesn't play bass like anybody else; he doesn't listen to the other bass
players, he listens to his head."[2] With Garcia and Lesh's influence, the
bands' philosophy was that there were no mistakes with improvisation,
only opportunities.

In November of 1965, the Warlocks received their first national attention. Jerry's friend David Grisman, a bluegrass musician, heard the band
play and mentioned them to writers for the folk magazine *Sing Out!* Grisman told the writers that the Warlocks were the best rock-and-roll band

he had heard in California. In the article, he mentioned one song he particularly liked called "Bending Your Mind." It just happened to be one of Garcia's original tunes.

Later that same month, the Warlocks had their first official photo shoot, which they hoped would improve their publicity. One picture from this shoot features a very young and clean-cut Bob Weir in the center, with Bill Kreutzmann peering darkly and almost menacingly over his right shoulder and a long-haired Phil Lesh grinning from behind his left shoulder. An unkempt Pigpen levels a serious gaze, sitting by Bob's right knee, while a clean-shaven Jerry, sporting a wedding band, looks on from the right corner of the picture at an angle that makes him symbolically appear to be larger than the others.

Shortly after the photo shoot, however, the band realized they would need to change their name because they were not the only group calling themselves the Warlocks. Phil Lesh discovered this when he came across an album by another band called the Warlocks at a record store. The group began to toss around a number of possibilities for a new name, from the Vikings to the Emergency Crew, the Mythical Ethical Icicle Tricycle, and His Own Sweet Advocates. None seemed to generate consensus or any measure of excitement. Then, in a dramatic act that was told repeatedly over the years, Jerry opened a 1956 Funk and Wagnall's *New Practical Standard Dictionary* and his finger landed on the words "grateful dead." Garcia later explained, "Everything else on the page went blank, diffuse, just sort *oozed* away, and there was GRATEFUL DEAD, *big* lack letters edged all around in gold, man, blasting out at me, such a stunning combination."[3] Grateful dead is a type of ballad or folktale about a hero who pays the debt for a corpse so that the burial can be completed, and then the hero later comes across someone in his travels who helps him with a difficult task or saves his life. This good Samaritan turns out to be the corpse. The Italian fairytale *Fair Brow* is one example of this motif. Jerry was not crazy about the name at first, nor were Kreutzmann or Weir, who found it a bit morbid, but people began to call them the Grateful Dead, and the name stuck. As they adopted this identity, the group was joining with an ancient storyline that existed from the time of the Egyptians, one that was related to honor and compassion.

DANCING IN THE STREETS

The Grateful Dead began to become more organized as their venues grew in size and number. They continued to play the Acid Tests, and Rock Scully, who heard the band perform during one of these events, became the group's first official manager. Scully had some prior management experience working with a group called the Family Dog. One of the first things Scully did as manager for the Grateful Dead was search for money to purchase a good sound system. The band had been using a borrowed system, and the sound was not particularly good. Scully approached Ron Rakow for the money, and Rakow attended a Dead show at the Fillmore. When he left the concert, he donated $12,000 to the band. Rakow knew they would never be able to pay him back, but he liked what he heard in their music and wanted to be connected to the Dead. Rakow remained a long-time associate of the Grateful Dead, advising them on a number of matters over the years.

In the summer of 1966, the Dead relocated from Palo Alto to San Francisco, and they began to play professionally in venues such as the Avalon Ballroom alongside bands like Jefferson Airplane. During this time, the Dead decided they needed a place where they could live and work together. They found the perfect place at Rancho Olompali, the site of the Bear Flag Republic Revolt of 1846 and the first battle of the Mexican-American War in California. Olompali was sacred land to the Miwok Indians who inhabited the area from about 500 a.d. The Grateful Dead called this place home for six weeks, enjoying the vast landscape, a large adobe house, and a swimming pool.

After arriving, one of the first things the group did was initiate their new home by holding several parties for all their friends. The first bash included a who's who of the San Francisco rock scene at the time: Janis Joplin, Jorma Kaukonen and his Jefferson Airplane band mates, George Hunter, Darby Slick, and Grace Slick, who was not yet a member of Jefferson Airplane, and David Freiberg, founding member and bass player for the band Quicksilver Messenger Service. Other notables attended, including Neal Cassady, Owsley Stanley, Rock Scully, and Danny Rifkin. It didn't take long for the place to be known for psychedelic exploration, communal living arrangements, and hippy philosophy. Girl Freiberg, an Olompali partygoer who was married to Quicksilver's David Freiberg, later explained the general sentiment of those she hung around with at the time:

> We felt that we were going to change this world to a better place. There are these wild theories being bandied about, for instance, Owsley used to say that there was some theory about how we had come from some other evolved planet and this consciousness had come to us, and there was a way to bring us to the next level and this was all brought to us from this outer

space place. That was a very Owsleyesque philosophy. But anything seemed possible. Sure, I was open to any alternative con-
cept of reality. I don't know that there is any real consensual
reality, isn't it all subjective?[4]

Among the Dead and their counterculture friends, there generally was
a distrust of the establishment accompanied by a pervasive apolitical, anarchist sentiment. Rather than foster hierarchies in the group, the Dead
thrived on a balance of power that permitted tremendous diversity among
them. Although many believed otherwise, Garcia did not consider himself the leader of the Grateful Dead; instead he was a member just like
the others in the band. Throughout the lifespan of the Dead, the band
was a shared responsibility among musicians and crew, and everyone contributed on stage and off stage. The staff members were partners in the
organization, and in time some held key management positions, including
Lawrence "Ramrod" Shurtliff, who cared for the drums and was president
of the Grateful Dead corporation, and Steve Parish, who took care of the
guitars and served as Jerry's personal assistant. Similarly, Garcia played
with his audience, never *at* them. To Garcia the audience was part of the
show, and while he was most often nervous before he went on stage, his
nervousness dissipated when he began to play. He tried to find someone in
the audience to focus on who had good vibes, which helped him through
the performance.

Garcia had a unique perspective on people and life that he developed
throughout his youth and young adult life. This philosophy guided his
work with the bands he was a member of as well as his music and art. Jerry
believed people should just be themselves and be happy. At the same
time, Garcia did have a vision for the world that he conveyed to others
and some hope for things to be different. He once explained, "We would
all like to be able to live an uncluttered life, a simple life, a good life . . .
and think about moving the whole human race ahead a step . . . or a few
steps."[5] Some refer to this outlook on life as a version of stoicism where
people recognize that most things are out of their own control and there is
little we can do to change our circumstances. Instead, individuals need to
have freedom to come to terms with what they understand and what they
do not. Yet this does not mean that people are free to do just anything they
wish. Jerry recognized that freedom came with responsibility, particularly
responsibility to your community. He also appreciated that there would be
times when individuals needed to figure out where they were going in life,
so there would be occasions when people made mistakes. Jerry believed
that anarchy and chaos and uncertainty led to new discoveries and new

forms of understanding. Jerry was not a fatalist; to the contrary, he tended to have a fairly optimistic and sometimes utopian outlook on life and a belief in focusing on the good that can happen. He explained:

> Essentially, I think that life is a progressive matter. Going through life you find that there aren't any true setbacks, you just continue to know more, to find more out. More stuff happens to you and more things become known to you. It's continual.[6]

Garcia explored psychedelics most intensely when he lived at Olompali. After this time, Garcia and the entire band backed off using psychedelics, although the influence would be long-lasting. When replying to a question about how psychedelics affected his music, Garcia noted:

> I can't answer that. There was a me before psychedelics, and a me after psychedelics; that's the best I can say. I can't say that it affected the music specifically; it affected the whole me. . . . I think that psychedelics was part of music for me insofar as I was a person who was looking for something and psychedelics and music are both part of what I was looking for. They fit together, although one didn't case the other.[7]

In spite of this, Garcia never thought of himself as a psychedelic musician, nor did he consider the Grateful Dead to be a psychedelic band; instead, they were rock band.

In June, the Dead relocated from Olompali to a former Girl Scout camp in Lagunitas. Big Brother and the Holding Company lived just five minutes away, and Janis Joplin, their newest member, began a romance with Pigpen, forged in part because of their shared love for the blues. Members of both bands became good friends. The Dead were busy doing gigs on most weekends, trying to make money on local band circuits. Things seemed to be going well for them overall, but they ran into some difficulties when they were not able to rehearse in Lagunitas because of noise. Jerry's childhood friend Laird Grant came to the rescue, finding them some rehearsal space in Sausalito.

As they practiced and performed in 1966, the Dead prepared for their first recording experience. They worked with Gene Estribou, who had a studio in his house just a few blocks away from the Dead's office at 710 Ashbury Street, Danny Rifkin's boarding house in the Haight-Ashbury neighborhood of San Francisco. They recorded "Don't Ease Me In" and

"Stealin'" from their jug band days, as well as an original tune by Pigpen and another by Lesh. The jug band songs were released on a 45 rpm record that sold only on Haight Street. Although the record did not circulate widely, the band tried to increase its fan base through a series of performances outside the Bay Area, including a few rough performances in the Vancouver area.

GOLDEN ROAD

Jerry and some other members of the Dead moved into 710 Ashbury Street in September of 1966. The large Victorian house had plenty of room for several people to cohabitate, and since the door was never locked, people moved in and out freely, including members of the band, Neal Cassady, and other friends and acquaintances. The band was financially broke, and the cheap rent and communal living on Ashbury Street allowed them to eat and survive. They helped one another, relying on the generosity of their friends and a shared commitment to their craft. For example, at one point, Jerry found a Les Paul Gibson guitar that he thought was perfect for him, but he didn't have the money to pay for it. Ron Rakow took Jerry to Dana Morgan's Music and gave him $900 to purchase it.[8]

The Grateful Dead became part of the political events of the late 1960s, placing them firmly among the counterculture movement. In October, California passed a law making LSD illegal. A demonstration called the Love Pageant Rally ensued. Organized by Allen Cohen, founder and editor for the *San Francisco Oracle* (a psychedelic newspaper in Haight-Ashbury), the Pageant confirmed that those in attendance disagreed with the lawmakers, and the participants wanted to make the point that they were not criminals because they chose to use drugs. Hundreds of people attended the event, including Ken Kesey, who was back in the United States from Mexico, along with members of the Merry Pranksters. The Grateful Dead participated in the event, performing on the back of a flatbed truck. This was one of their first free, outdoor concerts. Janis Joplin also entertained the crowd from this makeshift stage.

Open-air venues became one of the Grateful Dead's favorite performance spaces. Over the next several months, the Grateful Dead gave a number of free concerts. Some were in the Panhandle, where the Diggers, a bohemian group that combined street theater, art, and political action, gave free food away on a daily basis. Once after a riot on the Haight, the police shut down Haight Street, and the Dead took advantage of the moment to trick the authorities and play a free concert on a flatbed truck bed parked on the street. This later became known as the band's swan song to the Haight-Ashbury scene.

The early Grateful Dead shows had an old blues feel, primarily due to Pigpen's influence. Musically the band experimented with extended improvisations that linked songs together into seamless, epical pieces, mainly because the band just loved to play. There was an obvious influence of bluegrass and old stories in their music, particularly in tunes like Casey Jones and Candyman (see Appendix 3 for more information on select songs Garcia routinely performed). The band constantly innovated and tried different things with their music and sound, and if something didn't work out, they simply tried again. Robert Hunter and Jerry Garcia collaborated on most of the original songs the band performed. Hunter was the lyricist, and Jerry continually pushed him to get the words just right.

As fall turned to winter, the Dead became one of the most popular acts in the Bay Area, second only perhaps to Jefferson Airplane. There was a spirit and attitude in the Haight-Ashbury region that the Grateful Dead thrived on. The band provided a sound track to things that were going on in San Francisco at the time. Between October 1 and the end of December, they played the Fillmore Auditorium six times, the Avalon five times, the Matrix four times, and several other smaller venues. Although they were not wealthy, they were beginning to earn some money, enough to support themselves and some of their friends.

During this same time, Mountain Girl came back into Jerry's life. The two met for the first time a few years earlier when Mountain Girl was riding a bicycle in Palo Alto and heard banjo music coming from the Tangent pizza shop. She went inside to find Garcia upstairs practicing for a gig. Mountain Girl said hello, but Garcia, who was engrossed in his practice and running the same song over and over again, did not pay much attention to her. A few days later, Mother McCree's Uptown Jug Champions played at the Tangent, and Mountain Girl went to hear them play. She was not into electric music, and she seemed a bit annoyed that Bob Weir and Pigpen seemed to steal the show from Jerry, but she followed their music as the band played for the Acid Tests, forging a friendship with Jerry in the process.[9] Once she was back from Mexico with Ken Kesey and their daughter, Sunshine, Mountain Girl spent more time with Jerry, and their friendship grew into a romance. By the end of the year, Mountain Girl and Sunshine moved in at 710 Ashbury with Jerry and the others who were living in the house. Mountain Girl became an impressive force with the Grateful Dead, maintaining a much different relationship with the band than other wives and girlfriends did. Mountain Girl was tough and outspoken and she soon earned the love and respect of the band members.

In spite of his intensifying relationship with Mountain Girl, Jerry and Sara briefly considered getting back together around the time of Heather's third birthday. Ultimately they decided against it. Sara did not think 710 Ashbury was a place for her and her daughter to live, and Jerry continued his relationship with Mountain Girl.

CAN'T COME DOWN

As a prelude of the year to come in San Francisco, the Dead kicked off the New Year of 1967 with the Human Be-In in the Haight-Ashbury district. The Be-In was three days of rock music and psychedelic drugs that initiated what many consider to be the era of the 1960s, and it continued the October protest against the California law banning the use of LSD. The Grateful Dead performed on the back of two flatbed trucks in front of a crowd that some estimated was as large as 30,000 people. They kicked off their performance with the tune "Dancing in the Streets." A highlight of their show came when flutist Charles Lloyd joined the Dead onstage during Pigpen's number "Good Morning Little Schoolgirl." Other bands that joined the scene included long-time friends Jefferson Airplane and Quicksilver Messenger Service. Several speakers addressed the crowd, including poet Allen Ginsberg and Timothy Leary. It was here that Leary famously uttered the line: "Turn in, tune on, and drop out." The Be-In was a peaceful event with no arrests or other problems, and only two policemen watched the group from horseback. Phil Lesh later wrote that he felt quite privileged "to be part of something that was bigger and more important even than music: a community of loving, peaceful people gathered together to celebrate a new form of consciousness—one that I hoped would expand to embrace the whole world."[10]

The peaceful protest brought a great deal of national attention to the Haight and the counterculture it represented, and soon hoards of young people flocked to the region to experience this scene themselves. The Haight seemed to provide a respite and alternative from the challenges of mainstream American society, including the Vietnam War and civil rights strife. The media labeled these young people hippies, a derivation of the beatnik term hipsters, and the Be-In popularized the word in American culture.

Life continued as usual for the Grateful Dead in the immediate aftermath of the Be-In. They performed in local clubs, solidifying a loyal fan base in the region. As Garcia's talent became increasingly well-known in the Bay Area, fellow musicians called on him to help with their work. Jefferson Airplane was no exception. As Jefferson Airplane recorded their second album, *Surrealistic Pillow,* they sought Jerry's advice. He ended up playing on nearly every track of the album, providing an arrangement of "Somebody to Love" that propelled it to a number one hit. Jerry even named the album. For his contributions, the band listed him in the credits as a spiritual and musical adviser.

As Jerry wrapped up his work with Jefferson Airplane, the Grateful Dead started to cut their first album, titled *The Grateful Dead.* They worked with David Hassinger, the Los Angeles producer who also worked with Jefferson Airplane on *Surrealistic Pillow.* The Dead recorded the album in three nights, using speed and other drugs to keep them awake. The tunes they chose for the album were among the more popular pieces they performed at live shows, including "The Golden Road," "Beat It on Down the Line," "Cold Rain and Snow," and "Viola Lee Blues," perhaps the only song to sound as the band did at that time. The result was an album that clipped along at a very fast pace, too fast for Garcia to enjoy. The album cover contained another annoyance to Jerry. During the Acid Tests, Kesey dubbed Jerry "Captain Trips," a nickname that Jerry did not like. On the album cover for *The Grateful Dead,* Jerry was listed in the credits as "Jerry 'Captain Trips' Garcia." Warner Brothers threw a party for the band when the album was released; however, in spite of all the enthusiasm, the songs did not end up getting a lot of airtime on the radio.

In May, the band traveled to New York City, making their East Coast debut. They performed a free concert at Tompkins Square, followed by a paid gig at the State University of New York's campus at Stony Brook. Here they found enthusiastic fans who promoted their music across different campuses on Long Island. The band also had a week-long gig at the Café au Go-Go, an important venue for rock music in New York City, but they did not particularly like the space. The stage was small, the equipment did not fit particularly well, and, according to Mountain Girl, the place smelled pretty badly.[11] As the Grateful Dead performed, Frank Zappa's Mothers of Invention played upstairs, but Zappa was never a fan of the San Francisco music scene.

The Dead returned to San Francisco in time for the Summer of Love, which kicked off with the Monterey International Pop Festival—"three days of music, love, and flowers." Fifty thousand people turned out each day to see major music acts of the time including The Who, headliner Otis Redding, and Simon and Garfunkel, as well as rising stars like Jimi Hendrix and Janis Joplin. The festival was a peaceful event with no recorded arrests, and in many ways it set the standard for rock concerts to follow.

Organized by John Phillips of the Mamas and the Papas, and producer
Lou Adler, along with other rock stars of the time like Paul McCartney,
Brian Wilson, Smokey Robinson, Paul Simon, and Mick Jagger, the event
was pulled together in six weeks. The Dead and Jefferson Airplane almost
boycotted the festival because they were suspicious of the $400,000 deal
that Adler made to televise the highlights.[12] Owsley Stanley made a special batch of "Monterey Purple" LSD available to the concert goers, and
Adler had to ask him to not give it to the stage crew because he was afraid
the show would fall apart if they were taking LSD while they were running the lights and set.[13]

Twenty years later in an interview on NBC, Jerry recalled the first
Monterey festival and the fact that the Dead, as he said, "played badly
there, we played really badly there. That was one of our classic bad scenes."
The Who played the set before them and smashed all their instruments in
a dramatic finale of "My Generation," and Jimi Hendrix played just after
them, famously setting his Stratocaster guitar on fire during the set. The
Dead were not so dramatic. This festival began their "tradition of always
blowing the Big Ones."[14]

As Haight-Ashbury swarmed with more and more people in the summer of 1967, the culture changed. Tour buses started to bring in hoards
of people, and 710 Ashbury became a stop for sightseers because of its
famous residents. The police presence increased. Inexperienced young
people, bad acid, drugs developed in makeshift labs, and the introduction of heroin and amphetamines meant there was no turning back to
the more idyllic days when a small group of young adults hung out in the
Haight and attempted to make sense of themselves and the world around
them. Mountain Girl later reflected on the experience:

> We can blame the media. Media came to the Haight Ashbury
> in late 1966 and spring of '67 and were busily promoting the
> phenomenon of sort of a youth culture phenomenon in the
> Haight Ashbury. It was just barely there by the time the media
> got hold of it. People wanted to have an alternative to what-
> ever American culture was telling them they had to do at that
> time. In 1967, the Vietnam war had been going on, there was
> the draft. There was a lot of unemployment. . . . People weren't
> satisfied with the status quo thinking and wanted to grow up to
> be something different.[15]

Jerry thought the arrival of the Communications Company, a small news
operation on Haight Street, marked the beginning of the end. This com-

pany printed stories they posted around the Haight that contained bad news about people who were harmed as a direct or indirect result of drug use, casting a negative tone throughout the neighborhood.

As life changed in the Haight, the Grateful Dead continued to evolve as the members grew together musically. They returned to the east with concerts in Toronto, Montreal, New York City, and Ann Arbor. Mountain Girl and her daughter Sunshine joined the tour, and Jefferson Airplane was often billed on the same ticket as the Grateful Dead.

Percussionist Mickey Hart became a member of the band in September 1967. A stranger in a crowd during a Count Basie concert pointed Bill Kreutzmann out to Mickey Hart, and so Hart introduced himself to Bill. The two hit it off immediately, and they spent the evening after the concert drumming around the city on light posts and anything else they could find.[16] Hart's father Lenny was a rudimental drummer, which meant that he played in a marching-band style. Lenny won a drum championship at the 1939 World's Fair. Mickey's mother Leah was also a skilled drummer, and so it seemed natural that their son would be interested in percussion, even though Lenny left Mickey and Leah when Mickey was young. After a stint in the military, Mickey reconnected with his father, and they ran Lenny's music store in San Carlos, California, where they sold drums. But Mickey needed to be on the stage to release his creative energy, and after meeting Kreutzmann, he began to play with the Grateful Dead. The band's tendency toward improvisation was a good fit for him.

KEEP THE WATCH

The increasing police presence and authorities' efforts to crack down on the drug culture in the Haight made drug busts inevitable, and the house at 710 Ashbury was no exception. On October 2, 1967, a friend of the band who was under pressure from the police to help them make drug busts showed up at the house and asked if he could roll a joint. It was a setup he conducted at four other homes in the Haight-Ashbury area.[17] Eight narcotics agents, news reporters, and film crews raided the house without a search warrant, breaking through the front door after they were denied entry.[18] Band managers Rock Scully and Danny Rifkin, equipment manager Bob Matthews, Bob Weir, Pigpen (who never smoked marijuana), and six friends were arrested. Information on the band and the Haight-Ashbury Legal Organization (HALO), which was also located at 710 Ashbury, was confiscated. The group spent six hours in jail before being released on bail. They held a press conference the next morning where they discussed the problems with the drug laws and heightened police surveillance in the Haight.

Mountain Girl and Jerry were across the Bay in Sausalito when the bust occurred. A neighbor called them into her house when she saw them returning to Ashbury Street later that day. She knew there were still police milling around 710, and she was sure it was not safe for them to go back to the house. Thanks to her, the couple was not arrested. But Jerry and Mountain Girl never again lived in the house. The couple moved to the Sunset district with Sunshine, and then to a small cottage in Larkspur in Marin County, just across the Golden Gate Bridge from San Francisco. Other members of the band soon followed, also finding homes in Marin County. Joining them were hippies disillusioned with the scene at Haight. Many lived in small and sometimes abandoned summer cabins or outdoor camp communes.

Jerry and Mountain Girl were financially broke, and the cottage they rented cost them about $125 per month in rent. This was expensive for the couple and made it hard for them to make ends meet. They also needed a car since Jerry had to drive into the city for rehearsals with the band and for the evening gigs he played around the city. The couple had very little furniture or other amenities in their home, but that did not seem to matter to some thieves who broke in and took all they owned, including Jerry's banjo. Oddly enough, a few days after the robbery, the junkies who robbed them returned and allowed Mountain Girl to buy Jerry's banjo back for $90. Unfortunately, they never returned the baby crib, the diapers, or the other things they had stolen.

Other members of the Grateful Dead were broke too, even though they were performing a great deal. They started to realize that they were not particularly good at business decisions, in part because they felt that focusing on the business aspects of the band would somehow compromise their music. The Dead decided to hire a business manager to help them organize the financial aspects of their lives. Up to this point, Danny Rifkin and Rocky Scully helped as much as they could, but they were inexperienced with the music industry, and the band had fallen into terrible debt. Jerry explained:

> We were just happy freaks, man, we didn't know anything about money, or bills, or any of the rest of that stuff. It wasn't bad, though. Don't get the idea it was bad because it just wasn't real, and because it wasn't real was the reason that it got so? outrageously out of hand. And it wasn't until somebody started saying hey, listen, you guys are really in big trouble.[19]

That somebody turned out to be Lenny Hart, Mickey's father. Mickey suggested that Lenny should manage the band. Because Lenny had been a business manager and he was Mickey's father, the group felt they could trust him. Jerry seemed to think it was a good idea, and the other band members agreed. Jerry tended to be pretty laid back about management, and he understood that people made mistakes, so he was not too concerned with what was happening.

Work on the Grateful Dead's second album, *Anthem of the Sun,* began in earnest late in 1967. The band decided to take this album more seriously than the first, and they spent a good deal of time considering studios in Los Angeles and New York before settling down to do most of the work in San Francisco. They began working on the album with Dave Hassinger, who produced their first album, but Hassinger quit when he thought they were taking too much time on the project. He was frustrated by all the experimentation and suggestions that seemed far out, like those given by Bob Weir and Phil Lesh to record the sound of air. After Hassinger left, the band turned to Dan Healy, their soundman, to help with the tracks for the record.

The album became a hybrid of live performances and studio work. The band organized tapes from various live shows, sometimes playing four live performances of a song at the same time to create the sound they wanted. They worked with state-of-the art eight track equipment, adding in kazoos, trumpets, harpsichords and other instruments to create what Jerry later referred to as a collage. This was the band's first album with Mickey Hart on percussion and Tom Constanten on keyboards, and they both creatively influenced the studio work. Constanten became a permanent member of the band a year later.

The band often found it difficult to adapt to the constraints of working in a studio. Jerry described it as trying to build a ship in a bottle.[20] Instead, they thrived on live performances and the synergy between the band and the audience. The studio was isolated and limited in ways that live performances were not. But they did take advantage of the latest technologies by exploring the various sounds they could create in the studio, attempting to educate themselves about the recording equipment as they sought out effects that may not have been possible in live performance venues. Jerry later explained that this second album provided an opportunity for the band to try different things in the studio, to experiment. One experiment was an attempt to create stereophonic sounds. Mickey Hart moved around the studio with a drum around his neck hoping to give a special effect to the music. The album became a musical composition Jerry created with Phil Lesh, an album mixed for hallucinations. In the end, however, he was disappointed with the result. The effects he thought they captured in the studio did not come across on the album.

By this time, the Grateful Dead began earning a decent living on their live performances, and so they really did not feel they needed an album to generate more income. Their goal was not necessarily to become rich, but instead to play music for an audience. They continued to be deeply distrustful of the music industry, and they were not completely convinced an album would bring any benefit to them. The Dead knew their music did not fit the "Top 40" genre that was popular on radio, and the lengthy improvisations that marked their live performances would never be translated into the short pieces played on the radio, even on FM radio, which was becoming more widely used for alternative rock music. These factors led them to enter the studio on their own terms, and they were not particularly inclined to change their ways to work in the studio space. The band members continued to do drugs and approach music in an experimental and creative manner that was sometimes frustrating to the studio executives. When they finished *Anthem*, Warner Brothers studio executive Joe Smith sent them a letter to complain about their lack of professionalism. Smith wrote: "Your group has many problems . . . you are now branded as an undesirable group in almost every recording studio in Los Angeles."[21] This sort of reprimand did not concern Jerry or the other band members.

What did concern Jerry, however, was when someone in the band did not pull his own weight. As the Grateful Dead's music became increasingly complex, more and more practice was required of each member of the band. However, Bob Weir and Pigpen did not seem too concerned with this. Weir was not particularly interested in practicing, and Pigpen seemed to have some difficulty understanding the direction the music was taking. Jerry noticed, as did Phil Lesh, and when other strategies to change Weir and Pigpen's behavior did not work, they went to manager Rock Scully to have the two fired. However, the impact was insignificant, other than perhaps some hurt feelings; Weir and Pigpen refused to leave. Both continued to perform, but Pigpen began to play the congas and the harp more often, while Phil Lesh's friend Tom Constanten played keyboards in his stead. In time Weir began to practice more, and the band seemed satisfied with his efforts.

THIS TRAIN GOT TO RUN TODAY

By this time, the Grateful Dead began to tour more intensely. They played across the country, sometimes as headliners and other times opening for bands like Cream. In one adventuresome moment, they snuck into

Columbia University in a bread truck to play in front of the student union building, even though they had no real political investment in the student strike that had shut down the campus. The venues in which they played were often unruly and out of control. Because of their reputation, there were times when they were not permitted to play, including a free outdoor concert at Golden Gate Park they planned with Jefferson Airplane the day after Senator Robert F. Kennedy was assassinated.

The Grateful Dead's time on the road was raucous as they traveled by bus or airplane. The band did not have their own charter plane, so sometimes they had hundreds of pieces of equipment they needed to check in when they embarked on a tour. They were often rowdy on airplanes, engaging in pillow fights and goofing around with one another. United Airlines eventually banned them from the airline because their equipment and behavior presented so many problems, but they later rescinded the ban.[22]

As they traveled, the Grateful Dead often received stares or strange comments from people who were not accustomed to the long hair, strange dress, and weird behavior the band enjoyed. Jerry thought it was funny that they could shock people by their looks, and he found it amusing that some hotels would not accommodate them just because of their appearance or, after they became more well-known, their reputation. Once they stayed at a hotel, they often were not invited back because of the trouble they created playing pranks, being loud, and sometimes damaging the property.[23] The band members were living out a romance about being young men on the road in America, and they would not be dissuaded by conventions and social norms.

EVERY MINUTE IS A BRAND NEW DAY

Jerry and Mountain Girl left their Larkspur cottage for a new home in Madrone Canyon at the end of 1968. Robert Hunter and his girlfriend lived with them, and their long-time friend Janis Joplin had a house a few blocks away. The Garcia family stayed in this home for two years. Domestic life was fairly mundane. Jerry watched children's television each morning with Sunshine and he often practiced for hours on end, working with Hunter on new songs.[24] Band life seeped in and out of his domestic life. Jerry held vocal rehearsals with the band at his home, even though they had a building with an office in Hamilton Field that they used for a studio and rehearsal site.

Garcia soon began to play the pedal steel guitar, something he had wanted to do from his banjo-playing days. He approached the instrument as an experiment, trying things out and searching for a sound he liked rather than studying books about performance techniques. Garcia hooked up with his neighbor John "Marmaduke" Dawson, who played guitar, and the two began to perform together in a hofbrau house called the Underground on Wednesday evenings. David Nelson joined them, and in time the group became known as the New Riders of the Purple Sage. Soon bassist Phil Lesh was part of the group on bass, and Mickey Hart threw in on drums. One consequence was that, beginning later that year, the Grateful Dead had a new (somewhat overlapping) opening act that was fairly inexpensive to take on the road since there were only two additional members beyond the Dead. The New Riders typically played a 45-minute opening set with Jerry on pedal steel guitar, and then he would often play an acoustic set in between the New Riders and the Dead's electric set. These were long performances for Jerry. The Dead loved to play, and sometimes shows did not end until five or six in the morning. The band jammed for hours, fueled by the synergy with the crowd and the LSD.

The Grateful Dead released the album *Aoxomoxoa* in 1969, just a year after *Anthem of the Sun*. The album name was a palindrome created by cover artist Rick Griffin and Robert Hunter. For this album, the Dead used new technology, a sixteen-track recording device that intrigued them. This was the first album where Phil Lesh played acoustic bass, and the first album to mark the Garcia/Hunter partnership in songwriting. When they finished recording the album after nearly eight months in the studio, the Dead owed $180,000 to Warner Brothers, a huge sum of money for them, particularly for an album that would be their least successful on initial release. Jerry and Phil headed back to the studio in 1971 to remix the album, and the 1969 version was essentially lost. The recording included some of Garcia's favorite work, including "Mountains of the Moon," which includes Constanten playing organ and creating a calliope sound that Garcia loved.[25]

Recording for the third album, *Live Dead*, overlapped with *Aoxomoxoa*. *Live Dead* did not incur large studio fees because it was recorded during live performances. This double album, with songs "St. Stephen" and "Dark Star," helped the band to pay back the debt they incurred during eight months in the studio with *Aoxomoxoa*.

The Grateful Dead played 145 shows in 1969, but two were particularly notorious. In August, they agreed to play for a three-day music festival at Max Yasgur's 600-acre farm in upstate New York near a town called Woodstock. Thirty-two of the best known bands of the time performed for crowds that numbered as many as 500,000, in spite of the sometimes rainy weather and lack of basic amenities. The concert, billed as "three days of peace and music," was later considered to be one of the greatest moments of rock history, although few would have guessed it as the festival was getting underway.

The Grateful Dead were scheduled to perform on Saturday, after Santana, Janis Joplin, and Canned Heat. But the crowd was much larger than anyone anticipated, creating traffic, sanitation, and other problems, and the rainy and humid weather only complicated things further. The Dead took a helicopter from the hotel to reach the site of the concert because they could never get there on the highway, and then they experienced problems getting the equipment set up on the steel stage. Once they started to perform, the challenges intensified. Electrical problems created shocks when the vocalists neared the microphones. Phil Lesh's bass amp picked up signals from the helicopter radio creating strange sounds and distractions as they tried to play. It was pouring rain and the wind threatened to bring the stage down.

By all accounts, the Dead show at Woodstock was a disaster. Jon McIntire, who was the band's manager at the time, later recalled that as Jerry walked off the stage he said, "Well, it's nice to know you can blow the most important gig in your career and it doesn't really matter."[26] Garcia clearly recognized the significance of the event. He explained, "You could feel the presence of invisible time travelers from the future who had come back to see it, a swollen historicity—a try pregnant moment . . . as a human being, I had a wonderful time."[27] But that wonderful time was not caught on film because the Dead, always suspicious of anything related to major industry, would not sign the release for their performance to become part of the Woodstock movie. Neither would Jefferson Airplane. Instead they were left with their own memories of their lousy performance. Over the years, the band seemed to take some measure of delight in the fact that they played horribly at one of the most famous concerts of all time, and they often joked about this.

Then there was the Altamont concert. Originally, this was supposed to be a free impromptu outdoor concert at Golden Gate Park. The timing coincided with the Rolling Stones' conclusion of their U.S. tour, and when the announcement came that the Stones would perform, things began to unravel. Just 24 hours before the concert, the venue changed to the Altamont Speedway. The Dead had bad vibes due to the increasing disorganization of the event, yet no one anticipated how bad the scene would be.

The Stones hired the Hell's Angels to provide security for the event, but they were paid with 100 cases of beer and many of them came to the event drunk and unruly.[28] These Angels conducted themselves quite differently than the Angels who guarded the generators and electrical cords at outdoor concerts for the Dead at Haight-Ashbury. They had knives and were brutish, and soon things turned violent. Marty Balin of Jefferson Airplane was knocked unconscious during his performance when he attempted to keep an Angel from beating up a fan. Stephen Stills of Crosby, Stills, and Nash was bleeding after being poked by an Angel with a bicycle spoke.[29]

When they arrived at the scene, the Dead slowly began to grasp how serious the conditions were. The Angels set up their bikes in front of the low stage, a challenge to fans who tried to rush the stage (nothing was more important to a Hell's Angel than his bike). They had pool cues and other weapons to beat back any offender. As Jerry and Phil walked toward the stage, Phil turned suddenly, and his bass case hit Jerry in the face.[30] Lesh took this as a sign that things were amiss, and shortly after that they arrived, the Dead decided they would not perform that night, in part because they were concerned that their performance would only prolong the horrifying events that were unfolding.[31] When the Stones took the stage, the violence became much worse. Scores of fans were beaten and one fan was stabbed to death in front of the stage. Mick Jagger tried to get the crowd to end the violence, but to no avail.[32]

After the fact, there may have been some regret among the Dead that they did not play. Lesh explained that perhaps they were afraid at that moment "to stand up for our belief in the power of music and the spirit of our community to turn back the tide of hate and transform it into love."[33] Just two weeks after Altamont, the Dead produced a song "New Speedway Boogie" to capture their feelings about the unfortunate experience at Altamont. The song includes the line "Things went down we don't understand but I think in time we will."

SET UP LIKE A BOWLING PIN

The Grateful Dead traveled to New Orleans early in 1970 to do a series of shows with Fleetwood Mac and a band called the Flock. After the first show, in an unexpected yet not surprising turn of events, police raided their hotel and arrested the band and crew on narcotics charges. Pigpen and Tom Constanten were the only exceptions. Pigpen never used drugs, and Tom had recently converted to Scientology, which meant that he was no longer using either. In fact, Tom officially resigned from the Grateful Dead just before the New Orleans gig to explore different creative outlets for his work.

Louisiana had stringent laws about drug use, and the band members and crew knew that jail time was a real possibility. Lenny Hart posted bail almost immediately, including $3,750 that was not refundable, but the police still kept the Dead locked up for eight hours as they attempted to threaten and ridicule them.[34] The timing of the arrest came at a particularly inopportune moment for Jerry when he was in jail. Mountain Girl called the hotel to tell Jerry that she was going into labor with their first child, and the hotel clerk told her she would need to call the police station. Baby Annabelle was born the next day, but Jerry would not meet her until he returned home a few days later.

Jerry's family knew about his drug use, but there was not much they could do to intervene. As a nurse, Jerry's mother understood the dangers associated with drugs, but she did not worry about Jerry too much because she thought the drug use was just "trendy" and part of the music scene.[35] She never judged him, and she seemed to be proud that he was a musician. She even attended a few concerts with Jerry's brother, Tiff, although the music they performed was not her favorite genre.

Mountain Girl also did not judge Jerry because of his drug use. If anything, she understood why he was taking drugs. She once explained her perspective on drug use:

> I think that a lot of it is about having given ourselves permission to be weird. We gave ourselves permission. We also gave other people permission to be weird. Try to think outside of the box of convention. I think that's been terribly useful. As far as the drug culture is concerned, I think that's been terribly useful as well in promoting inventiveness in the arts.[36]

Drugs were part of life in the band and at home, incorporated into Jerry's everyday routines.

Shortly after the drug bust, the Dead went back to the studio to record *Workingman's Dead*, which includes the songs "Uncle John's Band," "Casey Jones," "Cumberland Blues," and "High Time." The album reflects in part the admiration members of the band had for the music Crosby, Stills, and Nash was producing at the time. The Dead decided to focus more on vocals on this album, which meant that they needed to tone back the instrumental work. *Workingman's Dead* also marked a return to more traditional American music as the band focused on storied songs that had connections to old-time music, which they performed on acoustic instruments only. *Rolling Stone* magazine readers voted it the best album of 1970, just ahead of *Déjà vu* (Crosby, Stills, Nash, and Young) and *Moondance* (Van Morrison). But the album also marked personal troubles for the band, including problems with their manager, Lenny Hart.

Different members of the band and crew noticed some unusual things about Lenny Hart's management of the band, but few questioned him initially. Finally, Mountain Girl, who was waiting for Jerry's payment for contributing to the sound track of a movie called *Zabriskie Point* so they could buy their home in Madrone Canyon, and Gail Turner, Lenny's secretary, went to Ram Rod, the Grateful Dead's reliable and much-respected crew chief. Ram Rod told the band that either Lenny went or he would quit the band, and Jerry backed Ram Rod. The band called a meeting with Lenny, giving him a week to present the books to them. After the meeting, Lenny went to Mexico, taking all the money.[37] Jerry's money was gone, and soon Mountain Girl was looking for a different home for their family.

After the confrontation ended, Jerry asked his friend Sam Cutler, a former road manager for the Rolling Stones and a recent addition to the Dead's road crew, to look into the Grateful Dead business to see how things were shaping up. What Sam found was not pleasant. Lenny Hart had set up the books and accounts in some unusual ways, and when it was sorted out, they realized that he had probably embezzled $100,000 or more from the Dead, although it was hard to know for sure. Mickey understood the band's decision and tried to help them through it, but it was incredibly difficult for him as he struggled with the losses his friends incurred because of his father. Mickey Hart decided to leave the band, and for the next five years, he struck out on his own.

The Grateful Dead continued to play concerts around the country, even in the midst of student protests against the war and other civil strife. They were empathetic to many of the causes but unwilling to make public statements in support of different groups, instead choosing to just play their music. Occasionally they played benefits to support particular issues, like the KPMX radio strike benefit, and sometimes they played free concerts to contribute some good will to the community. The Dead's music was well-received across the United States and in England, and they were in demand as performers.

At the end of June 1970, the Grateful Dead boarded a train dubbed the Festival Express. Joined by 140 musicians and their friends, including Janis Joplin, the Band, and Buddy Guy, they embarked on a tour across Canada. It was some of the best fun the band would have as they played with other musicians on the train, partying and having a grand time. But the concerts did not go exactly as planned. An activist group called the May 4th Movement (M4M) attempted to stop the concerts. The group was organized in honor of the Kent State tragedy, where members of the Ohio National Guard fired on university students, some of whom were protesting the American invasion of Cambodia. Four students were killed and nine injured. M4M demanded that the Festival Express events should be free to anyone who wished to attend. The first event planned for Montreal was cancelled, and the musicians moved on to Toronto. Here, numerous concert-goers were injured when 2,500 people tried to break in, and several people from the audience tried to make political statements on the stage. Jerry organized a free concert for 4,000 people to help ease some of the problems, but the damage had been done. Attendance at subsequent concerts was low, and they ended up stopping the train and the festival in Calgary, rather than Vancouver as originally planned.

Between August and September of 1970, the Dead recorded their fifth studio album, *American Beauty*. This record included well known songs like "Friend of the Devil," "Sugar Magnolia," and the autobiographical piece "Truckin'." Like *Workingman's Dead*, the album had a focus on vocals and songs more than the instrumental aspects of the music. Also like *Workingman's Dead*, this project was marked by tragedy. Phil Lesh's father died while they were working on this album, and Jerry's mother was seriously injured in a freak accident and died a month later.

Although Jerry did not have a particularly close relationship with his mother, he took her death quite hard. On the morning of the accident, she had taken her dog to Twin Peaks for a walk before starting her shift at San Francisco General Hospital. In the parking lot, she put the hand brake on the car, but the dog was excited and got between the brake and the gas pedal. In the confusion, Ruth ended up pushing the gas pedal, and her car went off the cliff into a tree. Jerry and Tiff went to the hospital every day for a month to see their mother, enough for Jerry to feel absolved by her.[38] Their relationship had long been strained, and Jerry experienced pain and guilt that their relationship was not different. Sara Ruppenthal Garcia visited Ruth when she was hospitalized, and Jerry took Mountain Girl there to meet his mother for the first time. They showed her a photograph of baby Annabelle who was seven months old. Ruth never met her.

According to Mountain Girl, Jerry was depressed after his mother's death, and he told Mountain Girl many stories about growing up and life with his mother. Jerry's memories were not always good ones. His mother was often busy running the business and she was not always available to her sons. Jerry felt that his mother should not have remarried after his father died, and he did not like that Ruth was buried next to Wally.[39] In the months following Ruth's death he seemed to throw himself even more deeply into his work, maintaining an intense performance and recording schedule.

In addition to touring with the Grateful Dead, Jerry performed in smaller, more relaxing venues with other friends on a fairly regular basis.

Jerry also continued to sit in on several albums his friends were producing, including Jefferson Airplane's album *Volunteers* and Crosby, Stills, Nash, and Young's album *Déjà vu*. Jerry's contribution is distinctive, particularly when he played the pedal steel guitar for the break in the song "Teach Your Children Well." Jerry began to play regularly with new friends like keyboardists Howard Wales and Merle Saunders, bass player John Kahn, and percussionist Bill Vitt. Soon Richard Loren began to manage the group, coordinating Jerry's schedule around Dead commitments by working with Sam Cutler, who was managing the Dead by this time. But Jerry was always itching to play guitar, and when the Dead came back from touring, he was eager to play at local bars with Merle, John, and other musician friends.

Some musician friends were neighbors to Jerry. When Jerry and Mountain Girl's rented Larkspur cabin went on the market, they moved to a small home in Novato, near David Freiberg's house. Jerry spent his time hanging out with Freiberg, Paul Kantner, and Grace Slick, or playing regularly at the Matrix with Merl Saunders, John Kahn and Bill Vitt. This latter group was his primary musical focus outside the Grateful Dead. Jerry later explained that he learned a great deal about music from Saunders, who taught him about standard musical forms and structures.

As 1970 came to a close, *Rolling Stone* magazine named the Grateful Dead "Band of the Year," and Garcia "Working-Class Hero." They performed 142 concerts, which would be the second highest number of shows in one year across the history of the band. They were not making much money at the time, approximately $125 per week for musicians, crew, and staff, but they seemed to be happy.[40] The Grateful Dead had a contingency of loyal staff and crew, and all involved enjoyed an open, trusting, and egalitarian relationship. The Dead continued to play long concerts and they generally had quite a good time in the process. The band was improving as musicians and fine-tuning their sound. Part of this fine tuning involved finding the right instruments. Jerry experimented with different guitars over the years, and he finally switched from Gibson guitars to a Fender Stratocaster, which was better for finger-picking and the country music he enjoyed playing.

NOTES

1. Dennis McNally, *A Long Strange Trip*. New York: Broadway Books, 2002.

2. David Dodd and Diane Spaulding, *The Grateful Dead Reader*. London: Oxford University Press, p. 18.

3. McNally, 2002, p. 100.

4. *SF Gate*, http://www.sfgate.com/cgi-bin/article/c/a/2007/05/20/MNSOL-BRIGDEN20.DTL (accessed November 24, 2008).

5. Horace Fairlamb, "Community at the Edge of Chaos: The Dead's Cultural Revolution," in Steven Gimbel (Ed.), *The Grateful Dead and Philosophy*. Peru, IL: Open Court Publishing, pp. 13–26, 2007, p. 13.

6. Garcia, Reich, and Wenner, 1972, p. 105.

7. Blair Jackson, *Garcia: An American Life*. New York: Viking Press, 1999, p. 106.

8. Greenfield, 1996.

9. Jackson, 1999.

10. Phil Lesh, *Searching for the Sound*. New York: Little Brown and Company, 2005, p. 98.

11. Blair Jackson, http://www.blairjackson.com/chapter_seven_additions.htm (accessed November 26, 2008).

12. Brian Hiatt, "Monterey Pop," *Rolling Stone, 1030/1031*, 2007.

13. Ibid.

14. Lesh, 2005, p. 106.

15. Joel Selvin, "Summer of Love: 40 Years Later," *SF Gate*, http://www.sfgate.com/cgi-bin/article.cgi?f=/c/a/2007/05/20/MNSOLGARCIA20.DTL (accessed November 26, 2008).

16. Lesh, 2005.

17. McNally, 2002.

18. Holly George-Warren, *Garcia: By the Editors of The Rolling Stone*. New York: Little Brown and Company, 1995.

19. Garcia, Reich, and Wenner, 1972, p. 75.

20. Jeremy Marre, *The Grateful Dead: Anthem to Beauty*. New York: Eagle Rock Entertainment, 1997.

21. Ibid.

22. McNally, 2002.

23. Jackson, 1999.

24. Greenfield, 1996

25. Garcia, Reich, and Wenner, 1972.

26. Greenfield, 1996, p. 117.

27. McNally, 2002, p. 335.

28. Lesh, 2005.

29. McNally, 2002; Jackson, 1999.

30. Ibid.

31. Jackson, 1999.

32. McNally, 2002; Jackson, 1999.

33. Lesh, 2005, p. 165.

34. Jackson, 1999.

35. Greenfield, 1996, p. 130.

36. Selvin, "Summer of Love: 40 Years Later."
37. Lesh, 2005.
38. Marre, 1997.
39. Greenfield, 1996.
40. Jackson, 1999.

Chapter 4

WATCH EACH CARD YOU PLAY

In the early 1970s, the Dead cut back on touring and the number of live performances, and in part due to manager Sam Cutler's skilled scheduling practices, they found they had more free time than in the past. Cutler began a booking agency, and two of the office staff started a travel agency, both for the Grateful Dead's operation. The band tried to strike a balance between work and other aspects of their lives so that they would still enjoy playing. But Jerry could not slow down; he was addicted to performing and so he continued to play in public as often as possible.[1] Jerry seemed to enjoy his time away from the Grateful Dead, engaging with audiences around different music and in smaller more intimate venues. Often stagehand Steve Parish would be with him, hanging out in the afternoons while Garcia practiced scales.

Touring was physically and emotionally demanding because the Grateful Dead played long shows, and increasingly the shows were selling out. Often not everyone who wanted to see a show was able to get in, and this created problems for the fans, something that bothered Jerry:

> In Boston we played for two nights and even so there were still about three or four thousand people outside each night that weren't able to get in because the place was sold out and the police maced them and did all that, it was . . . I mean you wonder, you begin to wonder why you're doing it if what you're doing is leading people into a trap.[2]

Fans who could not get tickets sometimes crashed the gates, causing distress to the band members who did not want anyone to be injured at their events. In time, the band worked with FM radio stations to broadcast their live performances so that fans who could not purchase tickets would instead be able to stay home and listen to the music. This also continued the trend of free concerts that marked their earlier years together, but in a different way as their music now could reach even broader audiences.

The Grateful Dead's fan base, the Deadheads, started to be a distinctive cultural phenomenon in the 1970s. In the album *The Grateful Dead*, the band asked fans to send in names and addresses so they could keep their fan base informed, and it did not take long for the Dead's office in San Rafael to be flooded with letters. Soon two people were put to work managing the mailing lists, newsletters, and fan letters. In time, the newsletter became known as the *Grateful Dead Almanac*. It is still being published with updates on former band members' performances and other activities.

Garcia understood that their fans were a uniquely loyal group who came to concerts in spite of the variability they may find in the performances. As early as the 1970s, there was a group of West Coast fans who attended every show. Jerry understood there was no good demographic description of the Deadheads. Instead, he pointed out that they came in

> all shapes and sizes and ages and occupations and endeavors and backgrounds and everything. The Deadhead is that person wherever they turn up in society that is looking for an adventure in America, you know, something to do that is not like everybody else does and the chance to get out and scare themselves a little.

He joked as the interview continued:

> We were amazed the first time there was more of them than us, you know what I mean?[3]

Parking lots outside the Dead concerts became a veritable marketplace for Grateful Dead cultural artifacts. Deadheads sold tie-dyed shirts, food, stickers, and other wares. Some people existed by touring with the band and selling their goods in the parking lot, and it became a symbol of solidarity with the Deadheads to buy these things and thereby sustain the Deadhead culture.

The Grateful Dead was known for challenging the mores and laws of society, and the Deadheads followed suit by creating their own economy and way of life in parking lots across the United States. The Deadheads were never a monolithic or easily definable group. Some seemed to be attracted to the Grateful Dead as an "outlaw band, and of a concert by the Dead as a place where the mundane reality of daily life is displaced by the sense that anything can happen."[4] Others found the culture less friendly. One fan who followed the band for seven years described the problems she witnessed:

> I came to take for granted that people would steal from a friend's backpack and rationalize their actions. I saw friends sleep with other friends' partners. I saw young women sexually assaulted after being unwittingly dosed with acid. I saw someone give a friend's dog acid just to watch it lose its mind.[5]

The fans who created problems at different venues because of poor behavior became known as "tour rats." This group created extensive controversy among the Deadhead community. To judge them and try to change their behavior would counter the philosophy that guided the Grateful Dead, but to allow bad behavior to continue was harmful to the community.

The Grateful Dead permitted their fans to make free tapes of the live concerts, a prescient act in many ways. Jerry thought it was a good idea to let the fans have the music. He explained, "As soon as we play it, we're done with it. Let 'em have it."[6] The tapes contributed to the Deadheads' growing culture and sense of community. As Deadhead Dan Hupert explained, the tapes provided "a compilation, every night of every show that went before . . . without a tape, what they played in Laguna in '68 is nothing more than past history. With it, however, it becomes a part of my present."[7]

As the Deadhead culture got underway, Jerry continued to play regularly with New Riders of the Purple Sage, and the group signed a contract with Clive Davis and Columbia Records, recording their debut album in December of 1970 and January of 1971. Around the same time, Jerry cut a solo album with a $20,000 advance from Joe Smith at Warner Bros. With this money, Jerry and Mountain Girl could finally buy a home of their own. Jerry later joked that the solo album begins with the song "Wheel" and ends with the song "Deal" because he was wheeling and dealing to get a house.[8]

Mountain Girl found the perfect home high on the hill in Stinson Beach, far from the Grateful Dead's office. It was the largest house in the neighborhood, with a swimming pool in the back yard, reserve land behind it, and stunning views of the ocean. A sign outside the home read

"San Souci," which means "without care." David Grisman and Richard Loren, Grisman's business partner, lived nearby, and they frequently visited Jerry's house in the morning to have coffee and talk about the music business. Loren soon came to manage Jerry's business affairs outside the Grateful Dead.

Grisman and Garcia forged a deep, life-long friendship. The two had much in common, including the fact that both their fathers were musicians, and both had died when the boys were quite young. Garcia and Grisman also shared a love for bluegrass music, and Grisman was perhaps one of the best mandolin players to be found. Once the two friends began to play together, they added Peter Rowan, who formerly played guitar for Bill Monroe, and John Kahn on bass. In time the group, whose members all had nicknames like "Spud" (Garcia) and "Dawg" (Grisman), became known as Old and in the Way. Soon they were playing bars, clubs, and bluegrass festivals, with Loren booking their gigs.

When Grisman visited Jerry, he often brought his daughter Gillian to play with Jerry and Mountain Girls' daughter Annabelle since the girls were the same age. Mountain Girl remembered this as an idyllic time in their lives. Jerry frequently watched television in the mornings with Annabelle and Sunshine, and at other times he sat in front of the television with the sound turned down while he practiced. The yard was beautiful and safe for the children to play, and Mountain Girl was able to tend to a garden. It was perhaps the closest the family would come to having a more conventional lifestyle, although theirs was still quite unconventional.

Jerry and Mountain Girl's new home had a small chicken house in the back yard that was converted to a guesthouse at some point, and Jerry soon renovated this into a small music studio. He worked on his solo album in this space, and then recorded the music in Wally Heider's Studio D. Jerry played all the instruments on the recording with the exception of percussion, which was performed by Bill Kreutzmann. The album sold well, particularly among Deadheads.

Garcia stopped playing with New Riders of the Purple Sage in the fall of 1971. The New Riders wanted to do more touring on their own, and they knew that Jerry would not be able to leave the Grateful Dead. Jerry understood that he could be compromising both groups if he continued on, and he felt that his pedal steel playing was not good enough for the New Riders anyway.[9] New Riders replaced Jerry with a steel guitar player named Buddy Cage, but Jerry still occasionally played with the group, contributing on banjo and piano to their second album.

THE WHEEL IS TURNING

The Dead toured Europe in 1972. Although they had played in England prior to this trip, that was an abbreviated visit. Now they were in Europe for a long, multi-city tour that included places like Copenhagen, Amsterdam, Düsseldorf, Frankfurt, Hamburg, Manchester, Paris, and more. Their concerts were well-attended, particularly in England and Germany, although the Dead and their entourage remained as unpopular with the European hotel staff as they had with their American counterparts.[10] Family members of the band, crew, and staff toured with them, including Mountain Girl, who particularly loved the hotel room they had in Paris.[11] Garcia and Hunter continued to write songs on the tour, the longest Grateful Dead tour ever, including the tunes "He's Gone" and "Brown-Eyed Women."

The Grateful Dead recorded the live European performances to use later for another album, *Europe '72*, a three-record set that sold quite well. When they were back in the United States, they set up the studio just as they had organized the stages in Europe, allowing them to recreate some of the feeling for the music and concerts. The overdubbing was particularly good on this album, and even allowed them to include Merl Saunders playing a Hammond B-3 organ. Willy Legate wrote the liner notes, where he explained his answer to the question: Why are the dead grateful?

> Because their presence is invoked. Acknowledgement of the dead is new life. All the living who have entered the mystery of the name of the Dead have begun to die. The gratitude of the dead is music.[12]

The album had good reviews, and it marked the end of the band's contract with Warner Bros.

On July 4, 1972, Ron Rakow, a long-time business associate of the Dead dating back to the time when he donated money for their first good sound system, presented a 92-page document called the "So What Papers" to the Grateful Dead, convincing them to start their own record company. The band had long been dissatisfied with their relationship with Warner Bros., primarily because they felt the company did not do enough to market their albums. In the end, they started two labels: Grateful Dead Records, which would produce Dead albums, and Round Records, which would produce work by members of the band playing with other groups. Clive

Davis, a visionary force in the record industry, also wanted to do records for the Dead, but Rakow won out. He became president of the new label. The relationship between Ron Rakow and the Grateful Dead was not completely rosy. He seemed to get along decently with Jerry, but he did not have the same regard from other members of the band.

THE EARTH WILL SEE YOU ON THROUGH THIS TIME

Jerry experienced deep sorrow when his friends and acquaintances in the music world died. He was saddened by Jimi Hendrix's untimely death in September of 1970, and he grieved deeply when his long-time friend Janis Joplin died from an accidental overdose in October of the same year, less than a month later. After Joplin's death, Jerry reflected,

> She was on a real hard path. She picked it, she chose it, it's OK. She did what she had to do and closed her books. I would describe that as a good score in life writing, with an appropriate ending.[13]

Hunter and Garcia penned "Bird Song" in her honor, which included the line: "All I know, she sang a little while and then flew on."

But no death affected him quite as deeply as losing his long-time friend Pigpen. Pigpen had suffered health problems for a number of years, first becoming quite ill in 1971. He had sclerosis of the liver and serious ulcers, health problems directly related to his drinking habits, including his penchant for cheap Thunderbird wine and Southern Comfort. Finally a perforated duodenal ulcer caused him to bleed to death on March 8, 1973 when he was only 27 years old. Garcia was devastated. Rock Scully commented that he had never seen Jerry more unhappy than he did after Pigpen's death.[14]

When Pigpen died, Jerry decided that it was the end of the Grateful Dead. Pigpen had been such a central force in the band, and Garcia did not think they could continue without him. Jerry had a complicated relationship with Pigpen over the years. On the one hand, he had enormous respect for him as a musician and friend, but there were times when their friendship was rocky, particularly when Pigpen did not want to practice to improve his playing in the band.

Two days after Pigpen's funeral, the band decided they must continue on, and Jerry conceded. Keith and Donna Godchaux had recently joined the Dead, with Keith on keyboards and Donna as a backup singer, and their presence provided new possibilities. The way in which the couple came to be members in the band is the stuff of dreams. Donna boldly approached Jerry backstage at a concert and told him that Keith would be the next keyboardist for the Dead. Jerry heard Donna out and gave her his phone number, and they met at the Dead's rehearsal space a short time later. After Jerry and Keith played for a while, Jerry called Bill Kreutzmann to join them. Soon Keith and Donna were on the road, touring and rehearsing with the band.

THE PRESIDENT COMES ON THE NEWS

While his personal life was devastated by Pigpen's death, Jerry did not let the political events in 1973 go unnoticed. Jerry and the Grateful Dead did not support Nixon's hope to be re-elected to a second term as U.S. President, but they also would not publicly support McGovern in his bid for presidency. When McGovern asked them directly to endorse his candidacy, telling them they would be invited to the White House if he won, the Dead explained that they could only do so if McGovern legalized marijuana.[15] Of course he would not.

The war in Vietnam waged on, causing deep divides among people in the United States. Many Americans did not support the war, and protestors called for unilateral withdrawal of troops. Some Vietnam veterans, including John Kerry, who would later become a Massachusetts Senator, also opposed the war. Kerry helped to organize the group Vietnam Veterans against the War, and he testified to Congress in opposition of continuing the war. These tensions played out in American culture, including popular music. While the Grateful Dead tended to avoid political statements in their music and concerts, other musicians spoke out openly against the war, among them some of the Grateful Dead's friends: Bob Dylan; Crosby, Stills, and Nash; Neil Young; Joan Baez; and Country Joe and the Fish. Jerry was clearly opposed to the war from the beginning. During an interview after the release of *The Grateful Dead*, he uncharacteristically explained his position:

> The war is an effort on the part of the establishment to keep the economic situation in the United States comparatively stable . . . would I go? I would not go. I am totally against war . . . I could never kill anybody . . . I don't feel like I'm any kind of subversive force, you know; I feel like an American, and I'm really ashamed of it, lately.[16]

In spite of a peace treaty signed in January 1973, the fighting in Vietnam continued. President Richard Nixon was inaugurated for his second term a few days later. But his presidency would soon unravel as charges of campaign fraud and other crimes were revealed as part of the Watergate Scandal. Jerry and Mountain Girl watched the Watergate Hearings on television,[17] which culminated with Richard Nixon's resignation from office on August 9, 1974. In the aftermath of Watergate, whistleblowers, those people who would give anonymous stories to news reporters, were given protection under the law, and Congress passed sweeping campaign finance reform in the aftermath of the scandal. Unfortunately, these events had a long-term impact on the American public. Distrust of government and disillusionment with the establishment grew.

The Grateful Dead album *Wake of the Flood* was released in the midst of these historic events by independent distributors in mid-October, selling more than 400,000 copies. The band earned approximately four times the money per album with their independent label than they had earned with their Warner Bros. contract, so even though the sales were about the same, their income from the album increased dramatically.

By this time, the Grateful Dead's shows began to fill large stadiums as thousands of people flocked to the concerts. With the Allman Brothers, who credited the Dead as one of their early influences, they were one of the most popular touring bands in the country. The Dead's concerts moved from small arenas, theaters, and small stadiums that accommodated a few thousand fans to venues like the Roosevelt Stadium in Jersey City, New Jersey, where 23,000 fans attended, or the Grand Prix Racecourse in Watkins Glen, New York, where 600,000 fans showed up to hear the Dead, the Allman Brothers, and the Band. The Grateful Dead had become a megaindustry. Garcia was not particularly enthusiastic about this, preferring as always to play for much more intimate crowds, but other members of the band wanted to keep going, so he went along with them. Garcia was also acutely aware that quitting would mean a lot of people who had been faithful to them would be out of work.

The early to mid 1970s also brought new technical challenges to the Grateful Dead as they played larger venues. They were never quite satisfied with the sound systems they were using, and they often experienced feedback and distortion. To resolve this problem, Owsley Stanley worked with Dan Healy, Bob Matthews, and other members of the band's sound crew to design what would become known as the Wall of Sound. The Wall consisted of 89 300-watt and 3 350-watt amplifiers that stood 40 feet high and 70 feet wide and could project sound up to a quarter of a mile away. Each speaker in the Wall projected sound for one vocalist or one instrument, providing more clarity. This was no small feat to transport and set up at concerts. It took four semi-trailer trucks and at least 16 crew members to transport the 600 speakers and accompanying equipment, which meant that the Grateful Dead needed two Walls: one would be in use, and the other would be on the road to the next venue so that it could be set up in time before the next concert began. The Dead performed approximately 40 shows with the Wall of Sound, a time that Phil Lesh later described as one of the most satisfying performance experiences of his life.[18]

Another challenge the Grateful Dead experienced related to their drug use. Many of the members of the band began to use cocaine in the early 1970s, and it changed the dynamic of the group in some negative ways as people became irritable and paranoid. Cocaine was also a drain on their finances and forced the band to make some decisions based on money, something completely out of character for the group.[19] Mountain Girl says it devastated their relationship:

> If anything ruined our lives, it was cocaine. Jerry and I had fights about it. Coke makes you think you know it all and it makes you shoot your mouth off and it makes you hate everybody the next day.[20]

They could not sustain a healthy relationship under these circumstances.

Jerry faced other difficulties in his personal life as well. He was charged with drug possession when the police caught him driving over the speed limit on the New Jersey turnpike. Jerry was arrested and released on $2,000 bail. During his hearing, a psychologist submitted a report to the court stating that Garcia was not addicted to drugs, vouching for him as a family man and creative person. The judge ruled that his one-year sentence was suspended and would be dropped after a year if he was not named in another criminal case.

In addition, there were some internal problems with the band. In January 1974, the Grateful Dead fired their manager Sam Cutler. There were disagreements about how money was being spent, including the tremendous resources required to move the Wall of Sound around the country. In order to support the staff and crew needed to move the Wall, the Dead had to play increasingly larger venues like basketball arenas and football stadiums. Other aspects of the tour grew exponentially as a result: more security was needed backstage, and there was too much detachment from the audience. Many members of the band and crew were using cocaine, adding to the negative climate and expenses. In addition to these problems, Cutler did not agree with Rakow's management of the record label.

In spite of all the turmoil, Jerry released his second solo album in 1974, which consisted of covers from other musicians and groups including Van Morrison, Chuck Berry, Smokey Robinson, and Irving Berlin. This release was followed by the Grateful Dead's second album under their own recording label, *Mars Hotel*, which sold 258,000 copies but had mediocre reviews. Complaints among Deadheads related to the fact that the album had no extended guitar solos, something many fans enjoyed.

Shortly after this, the Grateful Dead embarked on their second European tour, although this tour was much smaller and involved fewer people than the first tour had and was much less fun because of social problems among the group. They began in London and then traveled to Munich. Once in Munich, the band fired their management because of internal disagreements in part fueled by drug abuse, making the remaining three events in the tour quite challenging to coordinate. Drug use, particularly heavy cocaine use, interfered with the band's work and it seemed that the Dead was be destined for disaster. Some speculated that they would retire.

Things became even more difficult when they returned to San Francisco and began filming for a movie about the Grateful Dead in the fall of 1974. Jerry loved film and he had long wanted to be involved in filmmaking, and Ron Rakow convinced him to learn on the job through this film project. The documentary would be based on the upcoming Winterland shows. Although many members of the band, including Phil Lesh, and long-time supporter Bill Graham had reservations about the project, Jerry was set on moving forward.[21] After the Winterland performances, the Grateful Dead planned to take a break from touring and performing.

Given all the problems the band experienced over the past year, the crew wondered if the shows at the Winterland between October 16th and 20th would be the Grateful Dead's last, but the band treated the upcoming break as a much needed hiatus, even though many of them were uncertain about the future as well. Some of the crew members felt the band could not wrap things up without Mickey Hart, so they decided to call him to rejoin the group for what seemed like its final performance. Hart jumped in during the second set of the last show for the song "Playin' in the Band," and it seemed as though he had never been absent. But even with Hart's surprise appearance, the band did not play particularly well that evening. After three sets the Dead ended the performance with an a cappella version of "We Bid You Goodnight." It was not clear to the Deadheads what would happen next, and many stayed as long as they could after the concert to absorb the vibes from the show. Afterward, the *Village Voice* noted, "There are a number of reasons why the Dead are going into hibernation, and one of them is that they tried to run their revolution as though it were a celebration. It didn't work."[22] Perhaps the *Village Voice* had it wrong, but only time would tell.

YOUR RAIN FALLS LIKE CRAZY FINGERS

In 1974, Mountain Girl was expecting her second child with Jerry, but she was frequently alone as Jerry worked on his music gigs. Often he performed one night with the Grateful Dead, and then other nights with one of his smaller groups. If neither of these were options, he sat in with friends who were performing in town. When Jerry was home, things were not easy for the couple. Mountain Girl suspected that Jerry was seeing other women at times, but when the Dead went on their second tour of Europe, she knew something was seriously wrong. Jerry said uncharacteristic things to her, including disparaging remarks about having a family and how that would ruin his artistic career.[23] Unbeknownst to Mountain Girl, Jerry had begun a serious relationship with a woman named Deborah Koons. Deborah was a filmmaker, and she had met Garcia after a show in March 1973. The two first corresponded by mail for about a year and then reunited.

Deborah spent some time touring with the Dead in Europe, and she also helped Jerry and Susan Crutcher with the Grateful Dead's documentary film shot at the Winterland. This created some awkward situations when Mountain Girl visited Jerry at the film house as he worked on editing the movie. It seemed that everyone but Mountain Girl knew that Deborah was his girlfriend. Deborah appeared to be the exact opposite of Mountain Girl in so many ways with her black hair, black sunglasses, and black clothing. Deborah was not particularly popular among many members of the Dead band and crew.

Mountain Girl's trusted friend Sue Swanson was at her side when she gave birth to baby Theresa, who was nicknamed Trixie.[24] Mountain Girl struggled to get Jerry back with her family, but she soon realized it just was not going to work out, due in part to his drug use. Jerry moved into a house in Tiburon with Deborah, and after it was clear Jerry was not coming back, Mountain Girl bought a home in Oregon, using money she earned from a book she wrote about growing marijuana. She moved with her daughters out of the San Francisco scene where she stayed for just over a year before returning to the area. Jerry did not give Mountain Girl child support money during this time, and so it was a constant struggle for her to make ends meet.

In spite of the problems in his personal life, Jerry continued a very intense work schedule, going to Bob Weir's home studio to record the Grateful Dead's next album, *Blues for Allah*. This album fulfilled an obligation to United Artists, a deal Ron Rakow forged to help infuse some cash into the organization. Their own record label was not doing well enough financially, and this alternative seemed to be a reasonable solution.

When the Dead entered the studio, they had no real sense of what they wanted this album to be. Jerry described this as one of the more experimental albums the band put together as they worked to create new styles and define new spaces for themselves musically. The project took considerable time, with some reports indicating that the band once worked a 50-hour stretch without stopping. With Mickey Hart reunited with the group, they slowly worked out new music that evolved in part from Phil Lesh's interest in geomancy and the Great Pyramids of Egypt.

As *Blues for Allah* was unfolding, Jerry also played on four other albums that were being created at the same time, including Keith and Donna Godchaux's debut solo album, Robert Hunter's album *Tiger Rose*, Phil Lesh's electronic album with Ned Lagin called *Seastones*, and Old and in the Way's self-titled live album. By the time Old and in the Way's album was released, the group disbanded, but Jerry did not miss a beat. He quickly became quite involved in another group called Legion of Mary, which included Merl Saunders, John Kahn, Martin Fierro on reeds, and originally Bill Kreutzmann followed by Paul Humphrey on percussion. Before their first tour, Ron Tutt became the percussionist. The group had a jazzier sound than other Garcia-Saunders collaborations, and audiences enjoyed the music. The group toured the East Coast for three weeks in April of 1975, but Jerry could not escape his Grateful Dead fame. People approached him wherever he went, and Jerry eventually just stayed in his hotel to avoid the situation. In time, Nicky Hopkins came into the group on piano and the Legion of Mary was renamed the Jerry Garcia Band. The group toured quite a bit in November and December, and they contributed to *Reflections*, Jerry's third solo album.

The Grateful Dead movie also placed huge demands on Jerry's time. He wanted to be involved with the film editing, and he spent hours in the studio reviewing the video clips. While working on the film, Jerry was particularly fascinated by footage of Deadheads, something he was not able to see when he was backstage before a show.[25] Jerry also decided that the opening to the film should include an animated sequence with an Uncle Sam skeleton perched on top of a Harley Davidson motorcycle and several dancing bears (originally created in honor of Owsley "Bear" Stanley). This added both time and expense to the film, but in the end was one of the highlights. The film work cost a great deal of money and was completed in 1977, nearly two years behind schedule.

Although the Grateful Dead took a break from touring in 1975, they still gave four live performances, including a free concert with Jefferson Starship at Golden Gate Park, a benefit for the late poster artist Bob Fried's family, and a benefit concert at Kezar Stadium. The Kezar Stadium benefit was Bill Graham's protest after the City of San Francisco eliminated extra curricular activities from its school budget because of a fiscal crisis. Graham called the benefit SNACK (Students Need Athletics, Culture, and Kicks), and with the Doobie Brothers, Graham Central Station, Jefferson Starship, Joan Baez, Neil Young, Bob Dylan, Santana, and the Grateful Dead on the docket, he raised $250,000 for the school board.[26]

In spite of his intense work schedule, Jerry's drug use continued to worsen. In 1975, someone gave Jerry what he thought was opium, but he ended up smoking an almost pure heroin base called Persian and became addicted.[27] Around the same time, free base cocaine was introduced to the Dead scene, and it devastated many in the community. Jerry was always able to perform, but there were some changes in his personality that concerned his friends. No one could talk him out of his drug use, although many of his friends and family members tried.

After a year and a half respite, the Grateful Dead hit the road again, exploring ways to keep the crowds and their lives more manageable. They dismantled the Wall of Sound, which allowed them to reduce their road crew significantly, keeping only the original crew from the band's early days. Jerry had a renewed commitment to the Grateful Dead and its success, acknowledging that the band was something bigger than he was.

There were other forces motivating this tour. Ron Rakow created one too many problems over the years. He was not particularly popular with members of the Grateful Dead other than Jerry, and he sealed his fate with the group over a couple of issues. One was the production of the live album for United Artists based on the final Winterland shows. The recordings were a disaster, yet Rakow pushed the project through, even with objections from Phil Lesh and others. The result, *Steal Your Face*, is one of the band's worst albums.[28] The sound was not terrific, and many Deadheads felt that the song selection was not great. It was a critical and commercial flop.

Rakow also created problems for Mickey Hart as he recorded his solo album *Diga*. The final straw for Rakow came when he decided to bankrupt the Dead so that their contract with United Artists would be null and void, allowing them to sign with another company to get a cash advance. Although Jerry did not seem to think this was a bad idea, other band members did not go for it, and Rakow was fired.[29] When he learned that he was cut from the band, Rakow deposited a $275,000 check for the Dead from United Artists in his own personal account rather than the band's account. He later claimed that he needed this money to settle up the band's debt, but he kept the money for himself. Round Records, the Grateful Dead's independent label for solo projects, and Grateful Dead Records, the label for the band's group projects, both folded. The Grateful Dead no longer had their own record label. Jerry, who had been loyal to Rakow over the years, was depressed about what happened, but he did not stand up for Rakow against the other members of the band. It was not his way. At the same time, he never held a grudge against Rakow for what he did or the money he took. The band never recouped the money.

MIGHT AS WELL

The Dead kicked off a new tour, returning to the stage on June 3, 1976 with a concert at the Paramount Theatre in Portland, Oregon. Their first tour focused on smaller venues marketed directly to Deadheads on their mailing list, but by October they were doing shows at the Oakland Coliseum with The Who. Pete Townsend seemed to be amazed that the Grateful Dead could play three sets without a set list to help them know what was next. Bob Weir seemed to be interested in this idea and in spite of the band's objections, he tried using a list at the next show. Needless to say, it did not work. The Dead thrived on letting the concert flow from one song to the next at an easy pace determined by the crowd and the moment.

Now that they were touring again, the Dead needed to find a new record company. They decided to sign with Clive Davis at Arista Records, and their first album under this new label, *Terrapin Station*, was released in 1977. The Dead worked with producer Keith Olsen, who had also produced a Fleetwood Mac album, to create a more commercially successful album. Garcia particularly enjoyed the studio work on this album, frequently laughing as they dubbed songs and rehearsed to meet the high performance standards Olsen insisted on. Deadheads had mixed reactions to the album, and outside the loyal fan base, it was tough to get an audience in a year when punk and new wave music offered alternative genres, exciting audiences around the world. In spite of this, when the album was released, *Rolling Stone* magazine declared: "A NEW DEAD ERA IS UPON US." Arista picked up on this theme, using it to advertise the Grateful Dead's album.

The Grateful Dead movie opened on June 1, 1977. Predictably, Dead-heads loved it. Jerry had been stretched in new and unique ways as he worked long hours on this film, hoping to convey the complexity of the Grateful Dead to audiences. But the project took a toll on Jerry and the band, whose members were not always thrilled with the time or money the project involved. In the end, it cost $600,000 to produce the film, significantly more than the $125,000 Rakow projected at the onset of the project. As the movie opened, Garcia explained that it changed his outlook toward the Grateful Dead and helped him to better understand the band's value.[30] Initial reviews were mixed. The *New York Times* called the film monotonous, while the *San Francisco Chronicle* praised the open-ing animated sequence. The *Village Voice* honed in on Jerry, referring to prominence the ordinary faces in the audience had, and noting "Jerry no doubt considers each beautiful in its own way. Such soft-headedness is his fatal flaw, and such equanimity is the secret of his magic."[31]

Jerry's relationship with Deborah Koons, which had always been tumul-tuous, ended by 1977, and he moved temporarily into a room in Richard Loren's home. In August, Mountain Girl moved back from Oregon to the Stinson Beach house with Sunshine, Annabelle, and Trixie. A few weeks later, Jerry came to the door and asked to move back in with her. By this time Mountain Girl had already sold the Stinson Beach home, but she found a new place in Inverness in Western Marin County north of San Francisco. The home was equally lavish.

Soon Jerry began to work on his first album with the Jerry Garcia Band. This initial album included his friends John Kahn, Keith and Donna Godchaux, Ron Tutt, and Merl Saunders. Released in 1978, *Cats under the Stars* consisted completely of original tunes by Hunter and Garcia as well as originals by John Kahn and Donna Godchaux. This was Garcia's favorite album, even though it was ignored by many of his fans and was not a commercial success.

As Jerry's friendship with Keith Godchaux became increasingly strained, perhaps due to Keith's problems with drug abuse, Jerry decided to end the Jerry Garcia Band, at least for the time being. His attention instead turned toward the Grateful Dead's next album with Arista, *Shake-down Street*, this time with producer Lowell George, a singer-songwriter and producer who initially became famous as a slide guitar player in the band Little Feat. One of Garcia's original contributions to the album, the song "Shakedown Street," was a nod to disco, which was sweeping the country at the time.

In the fall of 1978, the Dead resumed touring for large, packed stadi-ums. They performed in front of 150,000 at the Englishtown Raceway in New Jersey, one of the largest East Coast concerts any band had ever given. Mickey Hart was still recovering from injuries suffered in a serious automobile accident earlier that year, and Donna Godchaux was very pregnant with her first child, but the concert was a huge success, with particularly good sound quality and no problems with crowd control.[32]

The four continued to the Uptown Theatre Chicago and more excitement. At one concert, Jerry was introduced to an intriguing young fan named Manasha Matheson. The two had lunch together the next day and remained in contact with one another after that through regular phone calls and visits at concerts. One Uptown Theatre show was cancelled because Bill Kreutzmann and Keith Godchaux had an argument, although it was not clear to anyone what would be so serious that it would cause Bill to fly home from the tour. The Grateful Dead seemed to be ready for a new adventure and in the spirit of their *Blues for Allah* work, they decided to take a trip to Egypt.

IF I HAD THE WORLD TO GIVE

As the band, crew, and families, an entourage of approximately 200 people, traveled to Egypt, President Jimmy Carter was meeting with Egyptian President Anwar Sadat and Israeli Prime Minister Menachem Begin outside Washington, DC to negotiate the Camp David Accords to further peace in the Middle East. Egypt and Israel were embroiled in a state of conflict beginning with the 1948 Arab-Israeli War, and neither country recognized the other. Resolution to the differences between these countries was difficult to achieve, but two peace agreements were signed September 17, 1978. One agreement, which dealt with the future of the Sinai Peninsula, which Israel captured during the 1967 Six-Day War, brought significant changes between the two countries. Through the Camp David Accords, Israel agreed to withdraw from the Sinai region, which led directly to the Israel-Egypt Peace Treaty that was agreed on in 1979. Israel was granted free passage through the Suez Canal, and the Strait of Tiran and Gulf of Aqaba became recognized as international waterways, furthering more peaceful relations between the two countries.

The Grateful Dead's trip to Egypt had been long in the making and included a great deal of negotiating between Grateful Dead representatives, including Phil Lesh, and government officials in the United States and Egypt. Lesh explained to the officials that when the band played in different contexts, their music changed, and they wished to understand the effects performing near the pyramids could have on their music. To seal the deal, the Dead agreed to donate all proceeds from the concerts to two Egyptian organizations: the Waf Wal Amal (Faith and Hope Society, a benefit for handicapped children) and the Egyptian Department of Antiquities.

The entire trip was enlightening for the Grateful Dead entourage. Mountain Girl later described one particularly memorable afternoon that she spent with Jerry, Mickey Hart, Bob Weir, and David Freiberg in the King's Chamber of the Great Pyramid. The chamber was deep inside the pyramid and built with bricks fit so precisely together that a piece of paper could not be inserted between them. Mickey Hart had a desert drum called a tar with him, and as he tapped out rhythms, the others hummed and sang, enjoying the resonant sound in the chamber. Dennis McNally later wrote that this was their favorite playground.

In spite of the provocative sites and sounds Egypt offered, Jerry struggled throughout the trip. He began to take painkillers and ended up sleeping quite a bit. He kept to himself and seemed unhappy, but he remained unwilling to talk about what was bothering him, even with his closest friends.[33] Yet he was still able to perform, singing in earnest to crowds with his long hair pulled into two curly pigtails. The Egyptians called Jerry "The Big Moustache."[34]

A Grateful Dead flag fluttered on a pole on the peak of a pyramid as the concerts unfolded. Each show opened with traditional Egyptian music as more than a thousand people filled paid seats close to the stage, and Bedouins and others listened free of charge from outside the fenced area around the pyramids. More than six hundred people performed in the concerts. As the shows transitioned from Egyptian artists to the Dead, Mickey Hart drummed along with the locals, and then Phil Lesh and Jerry joined in. Egyptian dignitaries, including Anwar Sadat's wife, attended the first concert, while many American and European fans found their way to the shows.

The last concert coincided with a lunar eclipse, a profoundly beautiful and enchanting moment. In spite of the incredible ambiance, the Grateful Dead were admittedly not at the top of their game. Some snags prevented the performances from being among the Dead's best. Bill Kreutzmann performed with one arm because his left wrist was injured. The piano tuner quit, leaving the piano very much out of tune during each of the three performances. Jerry later explained,

> Take a perfect setting . . . A total eclipse, a full moon, the Great Pyramid; everything perfect and we went and played shitty. It didn't really matter. We had a wonderful time, man, we really did.[35]

Although the tour was widely considered to be a success by band members, the Grateful Dead ended up half a million dollars in debt. To compound matters, the band had plans to use live recordings of the shows to create albums, but the quality was not strong enough to do so. Rather than continuing from Egypt to some shows in London as they originally planned, the Dead instead returned to the studio to finish recording *Shakedown Street*. They hoped to finish before their November tour, and in spite of the usual difficulties among band members, they succeeded.

Fifteen million viewers tuned in to *Saturday Night Live* on November 12, 1978 to see the Dead kick off the fall tour. It was their largest audience to date, and while Jerry was not a huge fan of television for performance venues, he played to the camera quite well. The band opened with "Casey Jones," followed by "I Need a Miracle" and "Good Lovin." They continued from New York across the country through mid-February 1979. While the performances were usually quite solid, the band suffered some personal struggles during this time. Jerry had bronchitis, and Keith and Donna Godchaux faced difficulties in their personal lives. Donna decided to leave the tour early, and Keith soon followed as all mutually agreed that their time with the Grateful Dead should end. Unfortunately, Keith was killed in an automobile accident just over a year later.

PARADISE WAITS

Brent Mydland joined the band as a keyboardist after Keith's departure. Mydland had been playing in Bob Weir's solo band, and he was familiar with the Dead's repertoire. Brent preferred the Hammond B-3 organ, and he used the instrument to provide a color and sound the band was seeking beyond the percussion instruments that typically dominated the band. Brent also contributed to the band's vocals by adding a solid tenor to the group's often shaky harmonies. Adding Brent and his talent to the group seemed to energize Jerry as new sounds revitalized their jams.

In the late 1970s, Jerry lived in a rented house in Hepburn Heights, San Rafael, California with Rock Scully, who became press liaison for the Grateful Dead. Jerry lived in the downstairs of the house while Rock Scully and his wife and two daughters lived upstairs. Many described this as one of the worst periods in Jerry's life. Scully was also deeply into heroin at this time, and Jerry's drug use worsened as he spent more time with Scully and John Kahn, both drug users.[36] During this period, Kahn formed a band called Reconstruction, which Jerry joined, and the two explored new territories in music as they attempted to bring jazz and rock together.

But the band lasted only nine months, something Merl Saunders attrib-
uted to Jerry's drug dependence.[37]

The ill effects of Jerry's drug use were also evident when the Grateful
Dead returned to the studio to record *Go to Heaven*, the first album with
Brent Mydland. Jerry was not writing music during this period, and he
had only three original tunes to contribute to the album: "Alabama Getaway," "Althea," and "What'll You Raise." But Jerry was not satisfied with
"What'll You Raise," and so it did not make it onto the album. The majority of the songs on the album were written by Bob Weir and John Barlow,
with a few contributions by Hart, Mydland, and Kreutzmann. The record
was finally released in 1980, behind schedule and to mostly negative reviews, but in time for the band's celebration of its 15th anniversary.

To celebrate 15 years together, the Grateful Dead performed in June
at the Folsom Field in Boulder, Colorado, and then they traveled to An-
chorage, Alaska where one of their shows coincided with the summer
solstice. They continued the celebration with a 15-concert stretch at the
Warfield Theatre in San Francisco. This was followed by two concerts in
New Orleans, and eight shows in New York City's Radio City Music Hall
in October.

While in New York, a decision was made to televise the Halloween
performance. Len Dell'Amico directed the recording, and in the end the
group decided to include writer-comedians from *Saturday Night Live* Al
Franken and Tom Davis. Both were Grateful Dead fans, and as hosts, they
integrated several funny backstage skits and a great deal of humor into
the telecast. The theme was a spin-off on Jerry Lewis's muscular dystrophy
fundraiser and was playfully dubbed "Jerry's Kids." In one scene, Jerry tried
to auction off his missing finger. Henry Kissinger joined the show, shocking the hosts with his supposed secret recording of the event. The band
played acoustic sets, including Mydland on a piano, offering a range of
older and new tunes to the audience.

Shortly after this broadcast, Len Dell'Amico began to work with Jerry
and the Grateful Dead on a music video *Dead Ahead*. Jerry seemed to
be much healthier and very engrossed in this project, but this would be
short-lived. By the middle of 1981, he was using drugs regularly again.[38]
While Jerry had successful performances in London and Essen, Germany
where they performed with The Who, he was disengaging from the band
and his friends outside of the performance venue. In spite of appearing to
be his usual gregarious self during interviews, the drugs, which resulted in
antisocial behaviors, were separating Jerry from people who cared deeply
about him. Jerry continued an intense and successful performance schedule with the Jerry Garcia Band, which had gone through many differ-

ent memberships between 1979 and 1982. One reason Jerry performed so much was to support his expensive drug habit, which could cost several hundred dollars per day.[39] His friends in the Grateful Dead were not able to do much to change Jerry's behavior and they were not in a position to tell him how to live his life. These struggles were largely unknown among the Deadheads, and few would have guessed the extent to which Jerry was struggling given the strength of the performances the band offered throughout the early 1980s.

On New Year's Eve in 1981, Jerry married Mountain Girl at Oakland Auditorium. They were married in Jerry's dressing room during a break in the concert. The ceremony, held in Tibetan, was conducted by a Buddhist monk who was Mountain Girl's friend. Mountain Girl was concerned that Jerry was going to die because of the drug abuse. She deeply loved him, and he loved her as well, but they had never before been married despite having two daughters and a long history together. Mountain Girl was hoping that the marriage would help to turn things around for Jerry. She did not condone his drug use.[40]

Before they married, Jerry was clear that they would not live together. He needed his privacy, in part because of his drug problems. After the wedding, Mountain Girl returned with her daughters to Oregon. Jerry stopped by to visit when he was on tour, and Mountain Girl and the girls traveled to San Rafael to visit with Jerry on occasion. In the end, the marriage did nothing to help turn Jerry's life around. Instead, Mountain Girl's worst fears were realized as Jerry's life spun increasingly out of control.

NOTES

1. Dennis McNally, A Long Strange Trip. New York: Broadway Books, 2002.

2. Jerry Garcia, Charles Reich, and Jann Wenner, Garcia: A Signpost to a New Space. New York: De Capo Press, 1972, p. 84.

3. "Jerry Garcia Micky Hart Interview 1987-07-07," MySpace.com, http://vids.myspace.com/index.cfm?fuseaction=vids.individual&VideoID=13477136 (accessed November 26, 2008).

4. David Fraser and Vaughan Black, "Legally Dead: The Grateful Dead and American Legal Culture," in Robert G. Weiner (Ed.), Perspectives on the Grateful Dead: Critical Writings. Westport, CT: Greenwood Press, 1999, p. 21.

5. David Pelovitz, "No, but I've Been to the Shows: Accepting the Dead and Rejecting the Deadheads," in Robert G. Weiner (Ed.), Perspectives on the Grateful Dead: Critical Writings. Westport, CT: Greenwood Press, p. 61.

6. Phil Lesh, Searching for the Sound. New York: Little Brown and Company, 2005, p. 174.

7. McNally, 2002, p. 385.

8. Ibid.

9. Blair Jackson, *Garcia: An American Life*. New York: The Penguin Group, 1999.

10. McNally, 2002.

11. Ibid.

12. McNally, 2002, p. 443.

13. John Rocco, *Dead Reckonings: The Life and Times of the Grateful Dead*. New York: Schirmer Books, 1999, p. 97.

14. Jackson, 1999.

15. McNally, 2002.

16. Ibid., pp. 186–87.

17. Robert Greenfield, *Dark Star*. New York: William Morrow and Company, 1996.

18. Lesh, 2005.

19. Jackson, 1999.

20. Ibid., p. 255.

21. Lesh, 2005.

22. McNally, 2002, p. 479.

23. Jackson, 1999.

24. Greenfield, 1996.

25. Jackson, 1999.

26. McNally, 2002.

27. Greenfield, 1996.

28. Ibid.

29. Ibid.

30. Jackson, 1999.

31. McNally, 2002, p. 502.

32. McNally, 2002.

33. Jackson, 1999.

34. Greenfield, 1996.

35. Jackson, 1999, p. 302.

36. Ibid.

37. Ibid.

38. Ibid.

39. Ibid.

40. Ibid.

The original Grateful Dead (L–R): Jerry Garcia, Bill Kreutzmann, Bob Weir, Phil Lesh, Pigpen. (Courtesy of Photofest)

Members of the Grateful Dead face reporters in San Francisco on October 5, 1967, following a police raid on their residence resulting in marijuana possession charges. From left: Bill Kreutzmann, Phil Lesh, Managers Rock Scully and Dan Rifkin, Bob Weir, Jerry Garcia and attorney Michael Stepanion. (AP Photo/FILE/Sal Veder)

*Jerry Garcia in Woodstock (1970), which was directed by Michael Wadleigh.
(Courtesy of Warner Bros / Photofest)*

Jerry Garcia performs in the 1970s. (Courtesy of Photofest)

Jerry Garcia, shown in 1994, a year before his death. (Courtesy of Rob Cohn / Photofest)

Chapter 5

BEEN ALL AROUND
THIS WORLD

I guess somebody up there likes me.

—*Malachi Constant,* The Sirens of Titan

The early 1980s continued at a hectic pace for Garcia on and off stage. He performed with the Dead and the Jerry Garcia Band on a regular basis, and sometimes he played acoustic sets with his friend John Kahn. *Run for the Roses,* a solo album, was released in October 1982. The album contained a mixture of songs that Garcia wrote with Robert Hunter over the years, but it was not commercially successful. The Grateful Dead remained busy with performances and a new project. In 1983 they founded the Rex Foundation to provide community support for creative endeavors in the arts, music, and education. The organization was named after a Grateful Dead Road manager, Rex Jackson, who had died in 1976. The band would set aside proceeds from six to eight shows each year to provide money for nonprofit organizations they felt were doing important work.

While public appearances seemed to be going well, by 1983, Garcia's health was declining significantly, perhaps speeded by heroin. During concerts, he did not interact with other members of the band or with the audience, he no longer smiled, and he seemed to stare at nothing in particular. When he was off the road, he did not take care of himself. He did not bathe and he did not eat well. He did not want to leave his house. His feet swelled and he had burn holes in his clothes from dropping cigarettes on himself. His friends worried that Jerry would accidentally start a fire. Even his brother Tiff was concerned:

There was a time in the 80s when Jerry was really reclusive, and I was pretty worried about him. I'd go see him and he'd be in this big house, downstairs in this small, dark room, and he'd never leave. . . . He wasn't lookin' good at all.[1]

In spite of his deteriorating health, Garcia continued to tour with the Grateful Dead, offering strong performances despite his poor affect. He reintroduced older Grateful Dead songs like "Saint Stephen" to the concert venues during this time.

By 1984, however, Jerry's health was in an alarmingly bad state. Friends and family members addressed him about his condition and encouraged him to seek help. They also tried to keep people away from Jerry who were bad influences. Alan Trist, who was addicted to cocaine, was fired from the band, and Rock Scully was sent to a drug rehab center and never returned to work for the Grateful Dead.[2] Since Jerry and Scully lived in the same house, many people blamed Scully for Jerry's condition because he was addicted to heroin too. Rock had long frustrated Sue Stephens, Jerry's assistant and bookkeeper, with his careless mismanagement of schedules and money when the Garcia band was on tour, and few were sorry to see him leave.[3] Jon McIntire, who had been working in St. Louis as a domestic violence and rape crisis counselor and also had training in chemical dependency, became the Grateful Dead's manager in Scully's place.[4]

But these changes did not have the impact on Jerry's life that his friends and family hoped. His daughter Annabelle recalled:

It got to the point where he'd call me up on the phone in Oregon and nod off while he was on the phone. . . . It was a long period of time my father wasn't himself at all.[5]

Friends were calling on Mountain Girl to do something about Jerry's condition, but he did not want help. Fame had also taken its toll on Jerry. He confided to his old friend Laird Grant, "This scares the shit out of me. Some people at the shows think I'm some kind of a f—ing prophet or something. That makes me crazy, man. I'm afraid to say anything because of what people are going to take from it."[6] Saunders later reported that it was harder than most people realized for Jerry to be part of the Grateful Dead.[7] Jerry once said of the Dead, "We don't want to be entertainers. We want to play music,"[8] but somewhere along the line they became entertainers and celebrities. The touring was taking its toll, and the fans were sometimes very difficult. Jerry locked himself in his hotel room or stayed alone in the back of the tour bus when they were on tour. He would have preferred to be anonymous so that he could walk the streets in cities like New York without being recognized, but he knew that was impossible.[9] Longtime friend and fellow musician John "Marmaduke" Dawson explained:

> He'd put up with all these hippies who would come in and lay their trips on him. Every f—in' hippie in the world wanted to talk to Jerry. They all had some cosmic things that they had to get him to explain to them or they had to explain to him. Everybody had to talk to Garcia, man.[10]

There were few places where he could have privacy, and the pressures that came with being famous weighed on him.

In spite of Jerry's popularity and the fact that millions of fans adored him, things continued to spiral out of control in his personal life. Led by McIntire, the Dead showed up at Jerry's house and demanded that he choose between drugs or the band.[11] Although this intervention was quite difficult for everyone, Jerry eventually conceded that he should enter a rehabilitation program. The band left feeling successful, but on January 18, 1985, a day before he was scheduled to enter rehab, Jerry was arrested with 23 packets of heroin and cocaine while sitting in his BMW at Golden Gate Park. He was parked in a no-parking zone. Some saw this as his call for help.[12] News of his arrest and drug addiction made headlines across the country, shocking some of his fans. Many Deadheads did not realize the extent of Jerry's drug problems. Jerry's lawyer was able to prevent him from having charges pressed against him, and Jerry entered a counseling program as part of the agreement his lawyer brokered.

About a month after the drug bust, Jerry returned to the stage with the Grateful Dead to celebrate the Chinese New Year. Rather than his usual black T-shirt, Jerry was wearing a reddish colored shirt, and he looked better than he had in years. While he had not yet beat his drug addictions, he was working on incrementally reducing his drug use.[13] Garcia was trying to change his life, and he relied in part on help from his live-in housekeeper, Nora Sage. Nora began to ration Jerry's drugs, cutting back on the amount he consumed little by little over a 12-month period.[14]

PAINTING IT LARGE

As he worked on kicking his drug habit, Jerry needed to find other outlets for his creative energy. He taught his cat to fetch,[15] and he returned to a pastime he enjoyed from childhood: creating visual art. Nora encouraged Jerry to paint, something he had not done since he was in art school, and he continued to be a voracious reader. Jerry needed to keep his hands busy, so Nora also found some kits for him to build remote-control cars, which he raced at a nearby park, and he also built model railroad set ups.

Some of Jerry's art was in small sketchbooks he carried with him. Jerry frequently doodled and drew during down times on tours and during rehearsals. The drawings seemed to flow effortlessly from his hand as the scribbles with pens and black ink slowly emerged into figures that were sometimes cartoonlike and other times more serious, depending on Jerry's plans and mood at the time. As might be expected, Jerry did not start at the beginning of the book with the first blank page and then work to the end. Instead, he opened the book to the first blank page he found and commenced his creation. Sometimes he worked on a page that was upside down compared to the other work in the sketchbook.

With his art, just like music, Jerry was interested in the effect that technology could have. Jerry experimented with a range of effects on a computer, and he sometimes finished his artwork using a Mac-based program called *Fractal Design Painter*. This program gave his work a 3-D effect. He liked the variety of colors and effects he could create on a computer.

As Jerry became more productive as a visual artist, Nora began to sell his work. By April of 1986, he was clean.[16]

I GO WALKING IN THE VALLEY OF THE SHADOW OF DEATH

In the summer of 1986, the Dead returned to the road. Jerry seemed healthier, and so did many members of the band. Bob Dylan and Tom Petty and the Heartbreakers joined the Dead on stage for some of their shows. Unfortunately, Jerry began secretly using heroin and cocaine on the tour, and to complicate matters, a dentist prescribed codeine to help Jerry when he suffered from an infected tooth.[17] Because the Dead performed to increasingly larger crowds, the concerts were held in outdoor stadiums, and the weather was often quite hot. At a July 7 concert in Washington, DC, the band performed in 100-degree temperatures and high humidity. Jerry became dehydrated during the concert, and he returned home the next day complaining of incredible thirst.

Two days later Nora Sage found Jerry on his bathroom floor moaning. She called 911. Jerry was immediately admitted to the hospital in Marin, and they were initially unable to diagnose what was wrong with him. The hospital did a CAT scan, but in order to keep him still during the test, they gave Jerry Valium. The doctors did not realize that Jerry was allergic to

Valium and shortly after they administered the drug, it caused Jerry's heart to stop. The hospital had to resuscitate him twice, and then he was on a respirator for more than 48 hours. Jerry also suffered kidney failure.[18]

Mountain Girl arrived at the hospital around 10:30 a.m. the day after Jerry was admitted. She was living in Oregon at the time and so she took a 6 a.m. flight to get to Jerry's bedside as quickly as possible. When she entered the hospital, the doctor told her Jerry was not expected to live more than an hour.[19] They had determined that he was in a diabetic coma. The doctors wanted to do a tracheotomy because Jerry was having trouble breathing and he was struggling against the respirator, but Mountain Girl would not let them. She knew that a tracheotomy would ruin Jerry's voice and that Jerry would never forgive her if she allowed this to happen. Even though the doctors prepared Mountain Girl for the worst, she believed Jerry would live.[20]

When it became apparent that Jerry would indeed survive, the medical staff expected that he would have long-term health complications from the coma. They did not know if he would ever walk again, and they thought he might have nerve damage and ongoing heart problems. But Jerry would prove them wrong. When he came out of the coma, the first thing Jerry said was, "I'm not Beethoven." It was a baffling message. Some weren't sure if he meant that he was not dead or whether he meant that he was not deaf and could hear what they were saying around him.[21] Either way, everyone was relieved to hear him speak.

Jerry remained in the hospital for four weeks as he recovered from the coma. Mountain Girl, Tiff, and other family and friends were a continual presence at his bedside. Tiff spent time reminiscing about their childhood, helping Jerry to recreate his memories. Jerry's daughters Heather and Annabelle met for the first time at the hospital, causing Jerry to cry when he realized how much they looked alike.[22] Hell's Angels took over security. In a gesture of goodwill, Steve Parish brought Jerry's guitar to the hospital room, but it was upsetting to Jerry because he was too weak to play.

When he was finally able to leave the hospital, Jerry returned to Hepburn Heights with Mountain Girl and his daughters. Nora was no longer his housekeeper. Mountain Girl and Laird Grant cleaned the house, getting rid of drugs that Jerry had hidden in all kinds of places throughout his home: in books, heating vents, and other secret hideaways.[23] Visitors stopped by to see Jerry, but he was not well enough to visit anyone for about three weeks. When he was finally strong enough to receive guests, Mountain Girl invited John Kahn and Merl Saunders to their home.[24] The two spent time talking with Jerry about music, which was just what he needed.

After a few weeks, Jerry's friends Len Dell'Amico, Annette Flowers, and Sue Stephens took Jerry to see a Los Lobos concert in San Rafael.[25] It was the first time Jerry was in public since he had left the hospital. He went backstage and saw Carlos Santana and some other friends he hadn't seen in a long time. Jerry began to dance during the concert, and then he went onstage and played a solo on the guitar. His friends were astonished, and they were so pleased. They felt that Jerry was back. After the concert, Len found him in the parking lot talking to some fans.

Shortly after this, Mountain Girl moved back from Oregon and bought a house with Jerry in San Rafael. Jerry was on the mend, and his daughters were glad to have his attention. Mountain Girl later remembered this as one of the happier periods they had as a family. Jerry was not doing drugs or smoking cigarettes, and it seemed that they had a lot to look forward to.

I WILL SURVIVE

From the fall of 1986 into 1987, the Grateful Dead became caught up in the energy from Garcia's healing. It was a time when the Dead took their music and performances to the next level. Bob Weir, Mickey Hart, and others stopped by to visit Garcia regularly, as did John Kahn, Merl Saunders, David Nelson, and Sandy Rothman. They encouraged Jerry to return to his music, and they spent time talking with him or going for walks. Guitar playing came back to Jerry more slowly than he would have liked, but with patient support from his friend Merl Saunders, he began to play again. It was not an easy process. Jerry had to relearn chords, techniques, and songs.

Jerry first returned to the stage on October 4 with the Jerry Garcia Band, performing in San Francisco. Mountain Girl worried that Jerry was not strong enough to deal with the rigors of public performances, but he needed money.[26] Soon after, Jerry joined the Dead on tour, and the band returned to the studio for the first time in many years to cut the album *In the Dark* for Arista. The song "Touch of Grey" was quite popular with audiences, and as Jerry sang the lyrics "I will survive," crowds cheered him on. In a public interview after Jerry's return to the stage, journalist Brian Connors asked Phil Lesh what the Deadheads could do to support the band. Phil replied by asking people to reconsider their use of drugs and not to use drugs anymore. While Lesh was not speaking on behalf of all the band members, it was a powerful and unprecedented statement that contrasted greatly with the earlier days of the Dead when the band would not tell anyone how to live. It is not easy to know how Jerry felt about Lesh's comment, but he certainly gave a different answer to the same question in an interview a month after Lesh's. He explained that he would never tell anyone what to do, nor would he expect anyone to change his or her behavior. He continued, "Everybody does what they want . . . I'm not tellin' people what to do, ever—man!"[27]

In spite of all his experiences and struggles, Jerry remained true to the beliefs he held as a young man in the Haight; that is, he still felt people should just be who they were. Garcia would certainly not become a poster boy for Nancy Reagan's "Just Say No" campaign against drugs, a television advertising campaign in the 1980s that was part of the Reagan administration's War on Drugs.

As the Grateful Dead hit the road again, they received increasing attention from a variety of sources. Phil Lesh referred to this time as the "MegaDead" era. Fans were more enthusiastic than ever, and the Deadhead scene outside concerts began to look more like a bazaar, as goods were sold and traded and people convened to socialize. San Francisco radio station KFOG aired the *Grateful Dead Hour,* hosted by Paul Grushkin and produced by David Gans. The show soon went to national audiences, fueled by Deadheads old and new. *Deadbase,* a publication that was a guide to shows and song lists, and *The Golden Road,* Blair Jackson and Regan McMahon's musicological analysis of cover songs with interviews of band members, experienced soaring sales. Ben & Jerry's Ice Cream released a new flavor, Cherry Garcia Ice Cream. Jerry was not supposed to eat ice cream because of his diabetes, but he was flattered. Initially, Ben & Jerry failed to ask permission to use Garcia's name, but after some negotiation, the ice cream company decided to pay Garcia a small percentage of the sales to use his name.

As the Dead tour continued through the spring of 1987, Manasha Matheson reentered Jerry's life with a force. She had been in the front row at Dead concerts for a long time. Jerry first met Manasha about a year after his relationship with Deborah Koons ended, and about three years before he married Mountain Girl at the concert in Chicago. Manasha's friends attended a Dead show the year before, and they took a pumpkin for Jerry with a note inside that read, "Manasha says hi!"[28] When Manasha and her friends went to the Chicago concert, they took a pumpkin Manasha carved. She gave it to Jerry before the set began, and then after the concert she went backstage to meet him. Jerry invited Manasha to the next show, and after the second show she went to a party at the hotel where Jerry was staying.

At a show in the Civic Auditorium in San Francisco, Manasha decided to cut her hair. Manasha had taken a class in living art, and she decided to put on a performance for Jerry. He thought it was funny. When the tour was on the East Coast in Hartford, the two talked on the phone and Jerry invited Manasha to visit. Manasha decided to go on the tour with Jerry, and she told him that she wanted to have a family with him.[29] Manasha was unpredictable, a quality that drew Jerry to her.

When the tour ended in Chicago, Jerry told Manasha that he loved her. Shortly after that, he sent her an airline ticket to meet him in Los Angeles. Just a few weeks later, Manasha announced that she was pregnant with Jerry's child. At first Jerry thought Manasha would be able to move in with Mountain Girl and his daughters, but Manasha decided to continue to live on her own.

WHOLE NEW VISION BORN EVERY NIGHT

Jerry was long interested in the combination of visual images and music. In 1986, he began to work with Len Dell'Amico on *So Far,* a 55-minute stream of Grateful Dead music accompanied by various visual images and effects. Songs were recorded against photographic images, film clips of dancers that were altered to create different effects, and 3-D images of tarot cards. The song list includes "Uncle John's Band," "Playing in the Band," "Lady with a Fan," and "Space," among others.

As the Dead launched its spring tour in 1987, Music Television (MTV) pursued a project with the band. Jerry really enjoyed the visual aspects of MTV, and he was intrigued by the project, but he also was a bit perplexed by the music that seemed to be popular on the television station. Heavy metal was on the rise in the 1980s, but when Jerry watched the guitar players on MTV, he could only say, "I don't get it. God, it's just so mindless."[30] But he continued with the creation of the music video, putting a decidedly Dead spin on it.

Gary Gutierrez shot the first Grateful Dead music video to the tune "Touch of Grey," which was a big hit with audiences. The video had full-sized skeleton puppets, manipulated by puppeteers at a live concert in Laguna Seca Raceway in Monterey. In the video, the skeletons, which were from a medical supply company and adjusted to fit the posture and height of each band member, were on stage and eventually transformed into the real band members during the last chorus of the song. One of the classic images from the video is when Jerry's skeleton turns into Jerry, and he shakes his head and sings, "I will survive."

After the "Touch of Grey" video, the Dead also recorded "West L.A. Fadeaway" and "Hell in a Bucket." Soon, MTV was airing "Day of the Dead," a 24-hour event where every third video was related to the Grateful Dead and there were video clips showing scenes from the parking lots outside Dead concerts. The event moved the band even further into the mainstream.

Despite more than two decades together, the Grateful Dead never seemed to tire of one another musically. In a July 7, 1987 interview on NBC news with Bob Weir and journalist Rona Elliot, Garcia explained that each night was different for the Dead and that is what kept them going. Weir noted that Jerry brought his bluegrass and country perspective to the music, while Weir brought space and jazz perspectives and Lesh brought orchestration. Jerry agreed that the different perspectives kept them motivated and interested, along with the fact that 80 percent of what the band did was improvised as they went along.

The summer tour brought record crowds, all cheering loudly to welcome and support Jerry and the Grateful Dead. The band was frequently on the radio and MTV, a constant presence in American life. The song "Touch of Gray" made it to number nine on the Billboard singles charts, the most popular Grateful Dead song ever. In the Dark climbed to number six on the Top 200 album chart. As the band continued to try to innovate, toward the end of the summer of 1987, Bob Dylan joined the Dead on tour. They spent several months rehearsing earlier in the spring, covering a broad range of songs, from early folk tunes to more popular music. But the concerts were often uneven as the Dead tried to play along with an often unpredictable and aloof Dylan.

As the Dead summer tour came to a close, Jerry embarked on a new adventure. He went to Broadway with the Jerry Garcia Band and the Grateful Dead to perform 18 concerts in the historic Lunt-Fontanne Theatre. The show was called Jerry Garcia, Acoustic and Electric, and it had the biggest first day sale in the history of Broadway. Six months later, Phantom of the Opera broke the record, but it did not diminish the popularity Jerry experienced at this time. Broadway demanded a grueling schedule, including five days where the groups played both a matinee and an evening concert. Jerry played an opening acoustic act with the Jerry Garcia Band, and after a short rest in his dressing room, which had once belonged to Vivien Leigh and Mary Martin, he returned to perform with the Grateful Dead. The show closed on Halloween night and Jerry returned to the West Coast.

Jerry and Manasha's daughter Keelin was born on December 20, 1987. Jerry seemed to be thrilled, and he promised to be more involved with Keelin than he had with his other daughters.[31] But Jerry began the New Year with Mountain Girl, Trixie, and Annabelle in Hawaii, rather than with Manasha and baby Keelin. Jerry loved to go to Hawaii, where he spent as much of his time as possible scuba diving. He took his daughters

Annabelle and Trixie with him on several occasions, as well as friends like Bob Weir, Bob Hunter, and Phil Lesh. Jerry even paid for his longtime friend Laird Grant to be certified in scuba diving because he wanted Laird to dive with him at night.[32] Jerry's daughter Annabelle explained that Jerry loved the freedom and beauty he experienced when he was in the water.[33]

Three months later, the Dead embarked on another huge and wildly popular tour in cities throughout the East Coast and the Midwest. Along with the popularity the band experienced came changes to the concert scene, most notably among the Deadheads. The younger members of the audience had not grown up with the band, and many did not necessarily understand the nuances of the music. Instead, they seemed to attend concerts to hear a popular song like "Truckin'," or to experience what they thought might be a 1960s style counterculture concert. These young people attended the concert alongside the older Deadheads, many of whom were professionals but still followed the band and its music, but the dynamics were changing in some disturbing ways. Many of the cities began to complain about the Deadheads and the problems that came as they surrounded the concert venues, and authorities began to target the shows to bust people for drugs, since they knew that illegal substances were likely to be used at the event. Several fans were incarcerated with lengthy sentences after being arrested at a Grateful Dead concert.[34] Jerry was deeply disturbed by this and proposed that they stop playing large stadium concerts, but to do so would mean they would make considerably less money.

In order to help compensate for these difficulties, the Dead began to send a small group into the crowd to teach them Deadiquette, or how to behave responsibly. The band understood the animosity the police and local officials held toward Deadheads, and already there had been deaths in the crowd. One young Deadhead named Adam Katz was a mystery, but many suspected that he had been killed by a security guard at a concert.[35] Another Deadhead, Patrick Shanahan, was beaten to death by Los Angeles area police outside the Forum when he sought medical attention.[36] The Grateful Dead felt responsibility and were devastated by these terrible events. The parking lots outside Dead concerts slowly came under better control. The crowd began to clean up its own trash and people worked to educate one another about responsible social practices.

The Dead played a series of concerts with other artists like Suzanne Vega and Bruce Hornsby at Madison Square Garden in New York to raise money and awareness about vanishing rain forests and the consequences this would bring. While it was out of character for the Grateful Dead to support a political cause, they believed problems caused by rainforest destruction were serious enough and life-threatening enough to warrant their support. After much research into various organizations, they decided the money would go to Greenpeace, Cultural Survival, and the Rainforest Action Network. This was the first time Jerry spoke out on a public issue at a large press conference, but he clearly felt strongly about the matter. He explained:

> We've never really called on our fans, the Deadheads, to align themselves one way or another as far as any political cause is concerned because of a basic paranoia about leading someone. We don't want to be the leaders, and we don't want to serve unconscious fascism. . . . But this is, we feel, an issue strong enough and life-threatening enough that inside the world of human games . . . there's the larger question of global survival.[37]

The benefit raised $600,000, and the *Blues from the Rainforest* album, with Merl Saunders and Jerry Garcia, followed.

I'D RATHER BE WITH YOU

In 1988, the Dead began to work on a new album, titled *Built to Last* after a song Garcia debuted on tour during the fall. The band first worked on the record at George Lucas's Skywalker Ranch in Marin County, California, and then in early 1989 moved to the Club Front to try some different techniques and technologies. They experimented with Musical Instrument Digital Interface (MIDI) technology, which allowed them to try different sounds. The album sounded like a live recording, and Garcia, who was one of the producers, seemed quite pleased with the outcome.

Soon the Dead began experimenting with MIDI technology in live performances as well. Garcia played percussion, pipe organ, trumpet, pan pipes, bassoons, choral sounds, and other sounds through his guitar to add special effects to his music. For someone who was truly enthralled with sound, these new technologies opened up endless possibilities for experimentation, play, and creative work.

The Dead toured extensively throughout 1989 with large venue shows on the East and West Coasts. Later in the year, Jerry decided to move from his home with Mountain Girl into a house in San Rafael. He began to spend more time with Keelin and Manasha, who still lived in San Anselmo. Jerry commuted between his home and theirs on a Honda motorcycle. He was able to disguise his appearance when he wore a helmet.[38] Jerry was trying to be a better father and become involved in little Keelin's life, and he seemed to truly enjoy being with her. His daughters with Mountain Girl were grown by this time. Annabelle was living in Alaska, and Trixie was taking classes in the East Bay. Jerry's friend and personal assistant Vince DiBiase, whose wife Gloria was Keelin's nanny, believed Jerry had great hope for his relationship with Keelin. He noticed that Jerry was a gentle and kind father, and that he was very proud of his young daughter.

But touring kept Jerry and Keelin apart more often than not, and the year 1990 brought little change to the Dead's extensive live performances. Jerry decided to move in with Manasha and Keelin, where he stayed until the end of 1992, so he could at least be closer and more involved when he was not on the road. Manasha toured with Jerry fairly consistently through 1993. In 1990, Jerry asked Manasha to marry him and she agreed, but the wedding never took place.

The Dead concerts in the 1990s added other new artists into the mix, including Edie Brickell, Bruce Hornsby (who played with the band off and on for about two years), Branford Marsalis, and old friends Crosby, Stills, and Nash. Jerry particularly liked how Edie Brickell could improvise while singing, and he proposed that they tour with Branford Marsalis, Bruce Hornsby, and Rob Wasserman with no musical material, only improvisation. But Manasha was extremely jealous of Brickell and put an end to Jerry's work with her and what would have been Garcia's Mystery All Star Darkness and Confusion Band.[39]

By the end of the 1980s, the Grateful Dead had become one of the top-grossing bands in the world, earning tens of millions of dollars in tour revenue in addition to the money they earned on record sales and merchandise. So many people came to depend on the Dead for their livelihood, the only way the band was able to keep up with rising costs and salaries was to perform more and larger venues, something that Jerry did not like but felt he could not stop. The band had to cover its $500,000-per-month overhead, and to do so they could only perform more. Jerry once explained the pressure this brought:

> We are a community, a family, a tribe. This pressure chokes off enthusiasm. It's killing [me] to keep doing the same tours. It has not much dignity. The pressure is so great that we can't stop. It's hard to be creative with a gun held to your head. It's a huge responsibility.[40]

When the band discussed taking some time off, Jerry worried about the workers. He pointed out that the Grateful Dead did not have enough money to survive financially if they took six months off, so they had to continue on.

The band and the Deadheads were having a great time throughout that summer, but unfortunately they were unaware that keyboardist Brent Mydland was struggling against drug abuse and depression. Two days after the summer tour ended, at just 37 years of age, Brent accidentally overdosed and died.[41] This was the third keyboardist from the Grateful Dead who met an untimely death. While Mydland's death was a shock to the entire Dead community, it seemed to hit Jerry particularly hard. Jerry reflected on Brent's death a year later in an interview with *Rolling Stone* magazine:

> Brent had this thing he was never able to shake, which was that thing of being the new guy. And he wasn't the new guy; I mean, he was with us for ten years! That's longer than most bands even last. And we didn't treat him like the new guy. . . . It's something he did to himself.

Jerry went on to contrast his own experiences with Brent's:

> I owe a lot of who I am and what I've been and what I've done to the beatniks from the '50s and to the poetry and art and music I've come in contact with. I feel like I'm part of a certain thing in American culture, of a root. But Brent was from the East Bay, which is one of those places that is like *nonculture*. There's nothing there. There's no substance, no background. And Brent wasn't a reader, and he hadn't really been introduced to the world of ideas on any level. So a certain part of him was like a guy in a rat cage, running as fast as he could and not getting anywhere. He didn't have any deeper resources.[42]

As they did in the past when Pigpen died, the Grateful Dead continued on. Bruce Hornsby became their keyboardist while they searched for Brent's replacement. Hornsby was a creative keyboardist who challenged and engaged Garcia in many ways, and he remained a guest with the Dead, performing with them on and off over the next few years. A few months after Brent's death, after interviewing a number of potential keyboardists, the group decided to bring Vince Welnick into the fold. Welnick formerly played keyboard for The Tubes and Todd Rundgren. He quickly set to work learning the extensive repertoire the band played, focusing primarily on using an electric keyboard and synthesizer with a variety of sounds.

In the fall of 1990, the Dead traveled to Europe to do a series of concerts and promote their new live album *Without a Net*. Manasha and Keelin traveled along, and they spent time with Jerry touring a number of famous sites like the Louvre and the Eiffel Tower in Paris. One photo from this time captures the young family sitting together with broad smiles. Little Keelin beside her father and Manasha's hand resting tenderly on top of Jerry's.

When Jerry returned to the United States after this tour, he reconnected with David Grisman, his Old and in the Way band mate. Jerry began to spend time at Grisman's studio, mostly playing an acoustic guitar, and the two began to record music that covered a range of genres, including original tunes like "Grateful Dawg." The recordings from this time capture some of Jerry's best acoustic guitar playing. Their album, *Jerry Garcia-David Grisman*, released in the spring of 1991, became a huge success with over 100,000 copies sold. Garcia even agreed to allow Justin Kreutzmann, Bill's son, to direct a video for the song "The Thrill Is Gone." Garcia and Grisman wore a suit and tie as they performed the song in a 1930s nightclub. By all accounts, the new decade seemed to be beginning well for Jerry. He seemed to be satisfied with his personal and professional life, but unfortunately this happiness would be fleeting.

NOTES

1. Blair Jackson, *Garcia: An American Life*. New York: The Penguin Group, 1999, p. 330.

2. Jackson, 1999; Dennis McNally, *A Long Strange Trip*. New York: Broadway Books, 2002.

3. McNally, 2002.

4. Robert Greenfield, *Dark Star*. New York: William Morrow and Company, 1996.

5. Jackson, 1999, p. 332.

6. Greenfield, 1996, p. 251.

7. Ibid., p. 141.

8. McNally, 2002, p. 315.

9. Jerry Garcia, Charles Reich, and Jann Wenner, *Garcia: A Signpost to a New Space*. New York: De Capo Press, 1972.

10. Greenfield, 1996, p. 163.

11. Jackson, 1999.

12. Greenfield, 1996.

13. Jackson, 1999.

14. Ibid.

15. Phil Lesh, *Searching for the Sound*. New York: Little Brown and Company, 2005.

16. Jackson, 1999.

17. Ibid.

18. Greenfield, 1996; Jackson, 1999.

19. Greenfield, 1996.

20. Ibid.

21. McNally, 2002; Greenfield, 1996.

22. Greenfield, 1996.

23. Ibid.

24. Ibid.

25. Ibid.

26. Jackson, 1999.

27. Ibid., p. 355.

28. Greenfield, 1996.

29. Ibid.

30. Greenfield, 1996, p. 242.

31. Jackson, 1999.

32. Greenfield, 1996.

33. Jackson, 1999.

34. For a detailed list, see David Fraser and Vaughan Black, "Legally Dead: The Grateful Dead and American Legal Culture," in Robert G. Weiner (Ed.), *Perspectives on the Grateful Dead: Critical Writings* (19–40). Westport, CT: Greenwood Press, 1999.

35. McNally, 2002.

36. "Fan at Rock Concert Killed by Police, Coroner Rules," *New York Times*, http://query.nytimes.com/gst/fullpage/html?res=950DE4DC1730F933A05751C1 96F948260# (accessed November 28, 2008).

37. "Grateful Dead/Rainforest Press Conference," http://forests.org/archive/general/gdrainf.htm (accessed November 28, 2008).

38. Jackson, 1999.

39. McNally, 2002.

40. Lesh, 2005, p. 298.

41. Jackson, 1999.

42. Holly George-Warren, *Garcia: By the Editors of The Rolling Stone*. New York: Little Brown and Company, 1995, p. 184.

Chapter 6

SHE BELONGS TO ME

In early 1991, Jerry visited with his first wife Sara and their daughter Heather. Jerry had not seen Heather since his hospitalization, and the reunion was at first difficult for him. It did not take long for the father and daughter to realize how much they had in common. Heather was also a musician, a classical violinist who played in chamber music groups and with the Redwood Symphony orchestra. Jerry planned to perform with the orchestra, arranging to write a few short pieces for guitar and orchestra. Unfortunately this plan never came to fruition.

The summer of 1991 Dead tour was hugely successful, but unfortunately Jerry was using heroin again. His drug use was evident as he again withdrew more and more on stage, even though his guitar playing remained creative.[1] When the tour ended, he entered a three-week methadone program in San Francisco. Methadone clinics are intended to provide heroin and opiate users with an alternative to these harder drugs with the hope that through counseling and maintenance on methadone, the addict can be weaned from drugs.

Shortly after the tour ended, on October 25, tragedy struck the Dead community yet again. Bill Graham was killed in a helicopter accident. Graham had become a top concert promoter across the course of his career, and he held a particular affinity to the Grateful Dead, booking them at the Fillmore West, the Winterland, the Shoreline Amphitheatre, and other popular venues. Many felt that it was Bill Graham who really gave the Grateful Dead their start, and he was a continual presence in their lives and career. Graham's death was another devastating loss for Jerry, adding to the personal pain he was experiencing at this time. The Dead participated in an outdoor concert at Golden Gate Park in Graham's honor, one of their largest shows ever. Soon after Jerry returned to the road with the Jerry Garcia Band; unfortunately, Garcia was provided with the drugs he wanted when he was on the road.[2]

OOO FREEDOM, OOO LIBERTY

In 1992, Vince DiBiase began to manage Jerry's artwork, which was getting more and more public attention. Vince cut things out of the sketchbooks that would be shared with the public and then sold the art. Some of his artwork was compiled in a book, *J. Garcia: Paintings, Drawings, and Sketches*. Art galleries all over the United States and in Japan began to display his work. Garcia was initially shy about his artwork, and he seemed to be surprised that anyone would be interested in it. Yet he soon came to understand that people were sincere. He was greeted with wide acclaim when he attended openings for his art shows.

Other commercial and creative deals were rolling in. Stonehenge Ltd. offered Jerry a contract to design neckties. He was not originally too pleased about this, but he eventually conceded. Jerry did not have any say in which designs would be used for the ties. The tie manufacturer used clip art to move a design from Jerry's artwork to the tie, and they used his signature on the label. These ties, which sold for about $28 each, soon became the number-one selling tie in the United States.[3] Over 150,000 of them were sold within months of their release. Celebrities and politicians, including Vice President Al Gore, were photographed wearing Garcia's ties, even though Garcia refused to wear one himself, even for marketing purposes.[4] But success with the necktie market did not mean that Jerry would produce other clothing items. He turned down a $5 million deal to design boxer shorts.[5] Book offers also started to roll in. Jerry turned down a three-book deal with Hyperion and Ten Speed Press to publish his art.[6] He also turned down offers to produce his autobiography.

Another creative outlet Jerry explored was film-making. Jerry always enjoyed films from the time he was a young boy, and he particularly liked to watch Scorsese films, and he enjoyed *Apocalypse Now*. Joining his interest in books and film, Garcia decided to buy the film rights to Kurt Vonnegut's second book, a science fiction tale *The Sirens of Titan*. A key message of this book is that life is the result of a series of accidents rather than the will of God. Garcia may have been able to relate to the main character, Malachi Constant. Like Malachi, there were certainly a number of accidents that shaped Garcia's life: losing his finger, his father's tragic death, the car accident that claimed Paul Speegle's life. Jerry seemed to resonate with this book on many levels. Garcia seemed to be most in-terested in the relationships in the book, particularly the relationships between the three main characters: Winston Niles Rumfoord, Bea Rum-foord, and Malachi Constant. One of the central themes of the book is the questioning of religion and human beings allowing themselves to be ma-nipulated by religion. The book also questions human pride, a theme that no doubt resonated with Garcia, who was known for his humbleness.

Jerry worked with Tom Davis and Richard Loren to develop the book into a movie. Hollywood did not like the script, and Jerry did not want to make changes. Finally Richard Loren and Jerry asked actor Bill Murray to read the book, and he agreed to work on the movie. Murray, Tom Davis, and Michael Ovitz signed a development deal with Universal to make the film.[7] But then Murray committed to do *The Razor's Edge*, based on the novel of the same name by W. Somerset Maugham, and Jerry's health de-teriorated. *The Sirens of Titan* movie was never completed, but Jerry loved the book and he paid money to keep the rights to the film for a number of years.

I ONLY WANTED YOU

Throughout the early 1990s, Jerry's personal life remained complicated. For one, Barbara Meier, Jerry's romantic interest from the days when he hung out at Kepler's Bookstore, reentered his life. She published a book of poetry titled *The Life You Ordered Has Arrived* (1989), and, according to Meier, after Jerry read the book, he wrote a letter to her claiming how he loved the poetry because it spoke from the heart. In the letter, he ad-mitted that he still loved her.[8] Jerry tried to see Barbara off and on during the two years after the poetry book was released, but the timing of their reunion never seemed to work out. But in May of 1991, Barbara finally met with Jerry backstage at the Shoreline Amphitheatre, and she later claimed that they picked up where they had left off nearly 30 years before. According to Meier, Jerry claimed that he thought of her every day and that he always loved her.[9]

On his 50th birthday, Jerry was on tour performing at Irvine Meadows in Irvine, California, but he was clearly not feeling well. He stayed in a hotel with Manasha and Keelin, explaining that he felt terrible, but he continued on to another show at Southwestern College outside of San Diego before returning to the Bay Area. When he returned from the tour, he moved into a house with Manasha and Keelin in Nicasio in western Marin County. The home was luxurious, with over 7,500 square feet on more than 10 acres of land.[10] Jerry had a large walk-in closet where he

kept his handful of black T-shirts, and he was looking forward to enjoying the swimming pool with his Newfoundland dogs.[11] However, within
a day of moving into their new home, Garcia became very ill and he
seemed to be slipping in and out of a coma. Manasha knew he would not
go to the hospital, so she called a doctor, Yen-Wei Choong, who practiced
Chinese traditional medicine. Choong prepared herbs, burned Chinese
incense, and gave Jerry acupuncture and tea. When he didn't seem to
improve, Manasha called Dr. Randy Baker, a Santa Cruz hippie.[12] Baker
and Choong cared for Jerry at home over the next several weeks, helping
him to recover. Jerry had congestive heart failure, along with emphysema,
a result of years of smoking. Emphysema makes it difficult to pump blood
into the lungs, and so his heart was failing as a result.

About a year after this collapse, Jerry discussed it with *Rolling Stone*
magazine reporter Anthony Decurtis. When Decurtis asked if Jerry was
concerned about whether his health problems would allow him to continue to do the things he wanted, and Jerry said that he was. He understood that he was not in very good physical shape and he was exhausted.
Decurtis continued by asking Jerry if he had been denial about the terrible
state of his health. Jerry admitted that he was:

> I'm basically a lazy f—. Things have to get to the point where
> they're screaming before I'll do anything. I could see it coming,
> and I kept saying to myself: "Well, as soon as I get myself to-
> gether, I'm going to start working out. I'm going on that diet."
> Quit smoking—*ayiiiiii* [*waves lit cigarette*]. In a way I was lucky,
> insofar as I had an iron constitution. But time naturally gets
> you, and finally your body just doesn't spring back the way it
> did. I think it had to get as bad as it did before I would get seri-
> ous about it. I mean, it's a powerful incentive, the possibility
> that, hey, if you keep going the way you are, in two years you're
> going to be dead.[13]

The health scare did result in Jerry changing his ways, at least for a
short while. With Manasha's help, Jerry quit using drugs, cut back on ciga-
rette smoking, went on a strict vegan diet, and began to exercise. Garcia
lost 60 pounds in five months as a result.[14] Manasha helped to manage his
health through careful attention to his diet and alternative medicine. Dr.
Baker recommended that the band tour less often and try to stay in the
Bay Area. Because of this, the Grateful Dead cancelled their late summer
and fall engagements, and the Jerry Garcia Band cancelled a tour they had
planned for November.

When the Dead started to tour again, Dr. Baker accompanied Jerry to Denver. Here, Jerry reunited with Barbara, who was living in the area, even though Manasha and Keelin were on the tour with him and the family was planning a trip to Hawaii. Soon Barbara began to travel frequently to the Bay Area to be with Jerry. It was a complicated time because Jerry was still living with Manasha, and he was still trying to be a good father to Keelin. At year's end, Barbara flew to San Francisco to be with Jerry, and Jerry decided to leave Manasha. He never said goodbye, although he told Manasha he loved her earlier that day; instead Jerry said he was going out to do some work and he never returned.[15] Vince DiBiase delivered a note from Jerry to Manasha, and he never saw her or little Keelin again.

Jerry and Barbara went to Hawaii for a month, spending three weeks in Maui and then another week on Big Island. Bob Hunter joined Jerry and Barbara in Hawaii, and the two wrote six songs together during this time. Jerry asked Barbara to marry him, but they were both married to other people (Jerry was still married to Mountain Girl at the time) and could not follow through on their plans.

When the couple returned to California, they rented a place in Tiburon. Jerry stopped smoking cigarettes for a period of time, and he walked for an hour every day with Barbara. Jerry seemed happier than ever as Barbara became reacquainted with members of the Dead and other friends she knew from their younger days. Jerry and Barbara even visited their former art teacher Wally Hedrick, where they enjoyed dinner and played music together.[16] Barbara was warmly welcomed by people in Jerry's life, including Mountain Girl, Sara, and Jerry's daughters. She seemed to be very good for him. Jerry began to write music again and seemed to be looking forward to the future with the Grateful Dead.

But the relationship was not to last. Soon it was clear that he was using heroin again. Barbara offered to help him through this time, but Jerry did not want her help.[17] As the Grateful Dead's spring 1993 tour began, Jerry told Barbara he was going to return to former girlfriend Deborah Koons. Jerry gave Barbara money so that she could pursue her interests in art and send her daughter to college, but the relationship was over. When they parted ways, it was the last time they would see one another. Soon Deborah joined the tour, although she was not particularly popular among the Dead band and crew. Some referred to her as "Black Deborah."[18]

One highlight of the spring tour was when the Dead visited the White House where Mickey and Jerry joked around in the Oval Office, sitting by the fireplace pretending to solve the world's problems.[19] They had dinner at Vice President Al Gore's home. The vice president and his wife Tipper had long been Grateful Dead fans. In fact, Al and Tipper Gore and one of their daughters attended a concert at RFK stadium just days before Gore was nominated as Bill Clinton's vice presidential candidate. Jerry respected Al Gore's environmentalist work, but he did not vote in the election.

When the spring tour came to an end, Jerry, Deborah, and some of their friends visited Ireland. Deborah was working on research for a film she wished to create that would be set in Ireland. Jerry was able to travel the country a bit more anonymously than he did in the United States. If people recognized him, they did not let on. Jerry enjoyed this time immensely, playing banjo anonymously for a group of Irish gypsies, taking in the sites of Galway, Connemara, Sligo, and the Burren.[20]

I WILL WALK ALONE BY THE BLACK MUDDY RIVER

As he resumed his relationship with Deborah, Jerry became increasingly isolated. Some attribute it to the people around him, like Steve Parish and Sue Stephens, who screened his phone calls and tried to limit access to Jerry, while others claimed that this was what Jerry really wanted.[21] People close to Jerry took care of his needs, including Steve Brown, Steve Parish, Jerry's personal manager, and Sue Stephens, his assistant. They screened his phone calls, and in many ways kept him isolated from the outside world and other people. They shopped for the dark-colored Levi's, corduroy pants, and t-shirts that were staples of Jerry's wardrobe. His favorite colors were black and blue. Those in Jerry's inner circle found houses for him to rent and paid his bills, and they also tried to protect him from the outside world, particularly when he struggled with drug use.

In the summer of 1993, Jerry spent time with his old friend David Grisman. They decided to work on a children's album called *Not for Kids Only*. The CD included old folk tunes like Elizabeth Cotton's "Freight Train," and classic children's tunes like "Jenny Jenkins" and "There Ain't No Bugs on Me." They included interesting sound effects like buzzing flies and mosquitoes. Grisman finished the album when Jerry returned to tour with the Dead. The album received strong reviews.

An art show featuring Jerry's work in Tokyo, Japan was scheduled to open on October 20, 1993 amid a great deal of hype. A Tokyo newspaper ran a full page ad to promote the show that said "Your Great Uncle Jerry is Coming," and a television commercial aired 10 times each day for weeks before the show.[22] Billboards all over the city promoted the event. Two days before the show, Jerry cancelled. He was tired and was not feeling well. The show went on without him, but there was no doubt that his fans were disappointed he was not there.

IF TROUBLE DON'T KILL ME, LORD I'LL LIVE A LONG TIME

By the end of 1993, Jerry's health began to decline significantly. He did not sleep; instead, he dosed off and on. He worked day and night. His divorce with Mountain Girl was finalized at the end of 1993, and Jerry had large financial commitments to meet as a result. Mountain Girl was given approximately $21,000 per month as part of the divorce settlement. In addition to this, Jerry paid Barbara Meier $3,000 each month for three years, and he also provided child support for Keelin and a large mortgage payment each month for Manasha's home.[23] Jerry had to keep working at a strong pace to keep up with these financial obligations as well as the costs associated with his personal habits and lifestyle, including the maintenance of his own home.

The new year began well for the Grateful Dead. They were inducted into the Rock and Roll Hall of Fame, but Jerry did not attend the events. The band had a large cardboard cut-out of Jerry they used at the press conference, and they reported that Jerry had a bad cold. But most people knew that Jerry generally did not like public awards and this sort of attention, so few were surprised at his absence.

Jerry seemed to be enjoying his time with Deborah. They traveled to Hawaii, and she accompanied him on tour. The two married on Valentine's Day 1994, but they continued to live separately. Jerry found a place on Audrey Court in Tiburon with a view of the Bay Bridge, San Francisco, the Golden Gate Bridge, and Mount Tamalpais, and Deborah stayed at her home in Mill Valley. Jerry's house was a "multisensory playground," with five televisions often turned on at the same time to different channels, two satellite dishes, and computer games. A sign above his computer read, "Nothing You Know Is True, but It's Exactly the Way Things Are."[24]

Jerry's performances through the spring on 1994 continued to be uneven. His playing was not always strong, and there were times when he forgot the words to the songs. When he was not playing well, he turned down the sound on his amp, creating an unevenness in the band's overall sound.[25] There were physical conditions in addition to his drug use that may have contributed. He was not able to sleep well, in part because of his longstanding struggle with sleep apnea. In addition, he suffered carpal tunnel syndrome, which caused him to lose feeling in the fingers of his left hand. His guitar was heavy and pulled on his left shoulder. By May, he was quite ill and collapsed back stage at the Desert Sky Pavilion in Phoenix, where he was performing with the Jerry Garcia Band. He refused to see a doctor, instead insisting that he just needed to go home. A private plane flew him immediately home. Jerry was supposed to travel with Deborah to Ireland, but Vince DiBiase convinced Jerry that he was too ill to go. Deborah went without him.

The Jerry Garcia Band had to cancel shows and tours because Jerry was too ill. But they played more frequently at the Warfield because it was near Jerry's home. When the Grateful Dead returned to the road for their summer tour, Jerry joined them, even though he was clearly in no condition to do so. Some of the road crew wondered if this would be Jerry's last tour, and others complained that it seemed they were only on the road for the money, a stark turn from their earlier days. The crew members were not the only people concerned about Jerry's health; Deadheads noticed how ill he seemed and wrote about their concerns in various Internet forums. When the Dead returned to perform four shows at the Oakland Coliseum in December, there were empty seats in the stadium, a rare occurrence for a Dead concert. In spite of all this, 1994 was the most financially successful year the Grateful Dead had. They earned $52.4 million from the 84 shows they played that year, as well as income from CDs and merchandise.[26]

IT SEEMS THAT ALL THIS LIFE WAS JUST A DREAM

By 1995, Jerry's diabetes was worsening, and it was rapidly increasing the problems he experienced with coronary disease. People with diabetes are not supposed to eat sweets, but Jerry continued to do so. Jerry did not want to monitor his blood sugar regularly, and his medical doctor did not think it was wise to give him insulin, which could be potentially deadly.[27] Dr. Choong left Chinese herbs for Jerry, but he would not take them. He had high blood sugar and high cholesterol, but he claimed that he felt fine. Perhaps this was because of the heroin. These health concerns may have slowed anyone down, but not Jerry. He began the yearly playing at the Warfield Theatre in San Francisco with the Jerry Garcia Band.

A few days after these shows wrapped up, Jerry Garcia was involved in a serious car accident. He crashed a BMW into a retaining wall while driving in the northbound lane of Highway 101 between Mill Valley and Corte Madera in Marin County. No one was injured, but the car spun around several times and finally stopped facing oncoming traffic. Jerry seemed uncertain about how the accident occurred and those close to him did not seem willing to claim that it was caused by drugs or his poor health.

Jerry's life with Deborah began to cause more concern among his friends and family. She fired Vince DiBiase and his wife Gloria. This concerned those closest to Jerry because they knew that the DiBiases looked after Jerry; in fact, Gloria was often the source of nutritional food for Jerry, and she frequently checked in on him throughout the night to be sure he was still breathing out of concern related to his sleep apnea.[28] But Jerry seemed to remain in good spirits despite these changes. For one, he was looking forward to his daughter Annabelle's wedding with some bemusement. When Annabelle introduced her fiancé Scott McLean to Jerry, he offered a good deal of advice about how to have a successful marriage. This mostly consisted of advice to not live together or spend time together. While he was pleased about Annabelle's upcoming wedding, he had learned some difficult lessons about being married.[29]

Jerry and Deborah vacationed in Bonaire off the northern coast of Venezuela in February, and when Jerry returned he was unable to play for the Jerry Garcia Band shows that were scheduled that spring. He was struggling with numbness in his hand. However, he was well enough to play concerts in Salt Lake City later that month, and he went on the Dead's spring tour through a series of southern cities. Jerry returned to the Warfield to perform with the Jerry Garcia Band in April, but he continued to struggle through the live performances.

Off the road, Jerry was working with Deborah on his autobiography, a picture book called *Harrington Street*. Delacorte Press paid him a six-figure sum to complete the book. It was a project he seemed to thoroughly enjoy as he reminisced on his childhood and experimented with different colors and art forms.

In June, Jerry was on stage with the Dead again, performing at the Shoreline. He seemed to be performing well, offering imaginative guitar playing and good vocal performances during the first two nights of the show. But the Sunday afternoon performance was difficult for him. There were equipment problems, and he did not play in sync with the rest of the band.

FARE YOU WELL

As his health continued to worsen, Jerry agreed to reenter rehab and get cleaned up, but he wanted to finish the summer tour with the Dead first. Jerry went on the road, beginning with a show in Highgate, Vermont. Bob Dylan joined the Dead onstage, but it turned out to be a bad scene. More than 100,000 people showed up for the performance, and not all of them could get in. As Dylan was playing, fans without tickets stormed the area, tearing down fences and opening the scene up for anyone who wanted to attend. Several fans were injured in the process. In addition, many of the fans were unconscious around tanks of nitrous gas.[30] The Dead were concerned that many of the concert-goers were not Deadheads, but instead just wanted to be part of the scene at an outdoor concert. Jerry and many others were concerned that the Deadhead scene was getting out of control.

The band continued to play large venues over the next several weeks. In early July, they were set to perform in Noblesville, Indiana at the Deer Creek Amphitheater as a benefit for the Rex Foundation. Unfortunately before the first show, there was a death threat on Jerry's life. Supposedly two men were in the crowd with guns. Phil Lesh and the others were willing to cancel the show, but Jerry would not hear of it. The FBI and the police were alerted, and undercover agents with tie-dyed t-shirts covering their bullet-proof vests attended the concert.[31] Metal detectors were installed at the gates, causing delays in the opening of the concert. As the show got underway, security guards moved closer to the stage. However, when they did this, the guards left a large portion of the fence unattended. Thousands of young people broke into the venue, and the police began to use pepper spray, tear gas, and German shepherd attack dogs to control the crowd. The second show had to be cancelled.

The Dead played Riverport Ampitheater in St. Louis three nights after the incident at Deer Creek. Fans who did not have a ticket crammed into the second floor of a pavilion during a rainstorm, and the pavilion collapsed. One hundred fifty fans were injured. Then the Dead went on to Soldier Field in Chicago to perform for more than 50,000 people as they sold out for the final stop on the tour. On July 9, the tour wrapped up. As Jerry left the stage he told Bob Weir, "Always a hoot, man. Always a hoot."[32] The Grateful Dead had given its final performance, although no one realized it at the time.

Jerry seemed to be happy when the tour ended, and he appeared ready to make some changes in his life. He took a week off to rest, and then checked into the Betty Ford Clinic to clean up. His decisions shocked many who were close to him. Deborah wanted Jerry to go to the Betty Ford Clinic, and the fact that Jerry actually followed through may indicate that he understood how seriously ill he was. Jerry spent two weeks at the clinic, where he went cold turkey off heroin, a very painful experience. The medical doctors put Jerry on medication for his heart, cholesterol, and other ailments. But Jerry did not stay at the center for the full treatment. Although he was supposed to be in rehab for a month, he left after two weeks. Jerry had instructions to follow up with a medical doctor to continue the various medications they prescribed; the doctors explained that otherwise he would die.[33] Jerry's years of drug abuse and smoking had taken their toll on his health, and his ongoing drug use likely masked how poorly he was feeling.[34] Unfortunately, it seems that he never followed up with a medical doctor to get the proper medications.

In the days after he left the Betty Ford Clinic, Jerry appeared to be doing well and conveyed an optimistic spirit to those around him. He visited the Grateful Dead's new recording studio in Novato, Kentucky Fried Chicken in hand. Jerry talked with Steve Parish and others about plans to build a guitar room in the new studio space.[35] He also talked with Bob Hunter on the telephone about working on *Harrington Street* and getting together to write some new songs. But once Jerry was off heroin, he realized how poor his health was and he knew he needed medical attention. He saw Dr. Baker again, but he was in a great deal of pain. The weekend after he left Betty Ford, Jerry decided to use some heroin to ease the physical pain he was experiencing. He explained to Deborah that his body was shot.[36] Some of his closest friends, like Alan Trist, felt that Jerry must have known he was going to die, and they thought he was taking care of things.

On August 8, 1995, Jerry checked into Serenity Knolls in a final effort to clean up. He did not tell a lot of people what his plans were. Many members of the Grateful Dead thought that Jerry was going to Hawaii to rest for a while.

Serenity Knolls is a 21-day treatment center. It is not a medical facility, and so there was no health examination when Garcia entered. Instead, he was put in a sick room for the first night so that he could be observed. After dinner with Deborah, Garcia went to his room and fell asleep. The staff reported that he woke up around 1 a.m. to use the restroom. When they asked if he needed anything, he replied that he did not. A few hours later, the staff found him dead in his bed, reportedly with a smile on his face. All efforts to resuscitate him failed. He had passed away a few hours before. An autopsy confirmed that Garcia died of a heart attack, a result of severe coronary disease.[37]

TURN AROUND AND I'LL BE THERE

Newspapers around the world conveyed the sad news that Jerry Garcia had died. Grieving fans soon gathered on Haight Street to mourn, while others congregated outside 710 Ashbury and in Golden Gate Park. A tie-dyed flag few at half mast over City Hall, ordered there by San Francisco's mayor. Fans gathered together across the country in various cities, including Central Park in New York City, while others shared information and grief in various Internet forums.

President Bill Clinton told MTV that Garcia was talented and a genius.[38] Vice President Al Gore eulogized Jerry, as did so many of his musician fans, from Carlos Santana to David Crosby, Branford Marsalis, and Bob Dylan. Unfortunately, those who knew him best were not surprised to hear that Jerry had died. Mickey Hart conceded that he no longer had to wait for this inevitable phone call.

On August 11, 1995, an open-casket wake was held for Jerry at the Saint Stephen Episcopal Church in Marin County. Only immediate family and band members attended, and Hell's Angels assisted with security. Deborah made decisions about the guest list, which included 250 people. Noticeably missing from the list were Mountain Girl, Manasha, and John Kahn. But John decided to attend the service anyway. Mountain Girl did not crash the funeral service as John did, but she did go to see Jerry at the church. Manasha did not try to attend the funeral either. She claimed that Jerry did not like big funerals, and she tried to stop the service from being open casket because she knew he would not have wanted this.[39] Rock Scully also believed that Jerry would not have wanted an open casket. There was an open casket at Pigpen's funeral, and Jerry reportedly told Scully he did not want this for his own funeral. It seemed the decision to have an open casket was orchestrated by Deborah, rather than according to Jerry's wishes.

The church where the funeral was held had stained glass windows with figures that were Gothic looking, reminding Sage Scully of the *Hundred Year Hall* Grateful Dead CD.[40] Before the funeral, Ken Kesey was in the parking lot giving people psychedelic drinks. David Grisman played "Shalom Aleichem" and "Amazing Grace," and he left a guitar pick in Jerry's pocket. Reverend Matthew Fox officiated the ceremony, and family and friends were invited to speak. Among the speakers was a very shaken Bob Hunter, who wrote a poem in Jerry's memory "An Elegy for Jerry." Jerry's daughter Annabelle told the crowd that Jerry "may have been a genius but he was a shitty father."[41] Her comment reflected the sense of humor she shared with her father, but was later widely misunderstood.[42]

Several other services in Jerry's honor followed. A public memorial was held at the Polo Field in Golden Gate Park two days after the funeral. People convened at the Haight and then walked to Golden Gate Park. There was a continual presence of about 25,000 people. A giant picture of Jerry was the backdrop to the stage. Mickey Hart arranged for some of the best drummers, including the Talking Drum percussionists from Africa, to attend. There was another memorial at Griffith Park in Los Angeles. Mountain Girl held a wake for Jerry at Alton Baker Park in Eugene, Oregon. Sara Ruppenthal held a Jewish shloshim service at her home in San Francisco.

In April of 1996, Bob Weir and Deborah Koons Garcia spread half of Jerry's ashes in the Ganges River in India. Some people were not sure why this was done, and the irony was not lost on Mountain Girl, who pointed out that Jerry never visited India and that the Ganges River was one of the most polluted rivers in the world.[43] The event was painful to Jerry's daughters, who heard about this through the news rather than from Weir or Deborah.[44] The remaining half of Jerry's ashes were sprinkled under the Golden Gate Bridge in the San Francisco Bay. Jerry's daughters Heather, Annabelle, and Trixie were there, as was Sunshine Kesey, Bob Weir, Phil and Jill Lesh, Tiff Garcia, Sue Stephens, Laird Grant, and Steve Parish. Deborah did not allow Mountain Girl on the boat.[45] The Bay was particularly rough that day, and as the ashes were spread into the water, some stuck to the side of the boat. Jill Lesh, Phil's wife, gave Bob a paper napkin, and he wiped the ashes from the side of the boat, nearly falling into the water in the process. A while later, Jill found the napkin with the ashes in her pocket when she was on a school field trip with her son Grahame. She spontaneously decided to bury the ash-covered napkin in the garlic patch she was helping the children to weed.[46]

Jerry's addictions were certainly difficult to understand, and the consequences were devastating to family, friends, and fans around the world, but he "was vital and true to himself up to the end. . . . He was *organic* through and through. It was always about the Band."[47] In his last interview with *Rolling Stone* magazine, he explained:

> I definitely have a component in my personality which is not exactly self-destructive, but it's certainly ornery. . . . It's like . . . "Try to get healthy"—"F— you, man" . . . I don't know what it comes from. I've always clung to it, see, because I felt it's part of what makes me *me*. Being anarchic, having that anarchist streak, severs me on other levels—artistically, certainly. So I don't want to eliminate that aspect of my personality. But I see that on some levels it's working against me.[48]

NOTES

1. Blair Jackson, *Garcia: An American Life*. New York: The Penguin Group, 1999.

2. Robert Greenfield, *Dark Star*. New York: William Morrow and Company, 1996.

3. Ibid.

4. Robert G. Weiner, *Perspectives on the Grateful Dead: Critical Writings*. Westport, CT: Greenwood Press, 1999.

5. Greenfield, 1996.

6. Ibid.

7. Ibid.

8. Ibid.

9. Ibid.

10. Jackson, 1999.

11. Phil Lesh, *Searching for the Sound*. New York: Little Brown and Company, 2005.

12. Dennis McNally, *A Long Strange Trip*. New York: Broadway Books, 2002.

13. Holly George-Warren, *Garcia: By the Editors of The Rolling Stone*. New York: Little Brown and Company, 1995, p. 200.

14. Jackson, 1999.

15. Greenfield, 1996.

16. Blair Jackson, http://www.blairjackson.com/chapter_twentyone_additions.htm (accessed November 28, 2008).

17. Jackson, 1999.

18. Jackson, 1999.

19. Lesh, 2005.

20. McNally, 2002.

21. Greenfield, 1996.

22. Ibid.

23. Jackson, 1999.

24. McNally, 2002, p. 607.

25. Jackson, 1999.

26. Ibid.

27. Greenfield, 1996.

28. Lesh, 2005.

29. Jackson, 1999.

30. Greenfield, 1996.

31. Ibid.

32. McNally, 2002, p. 612.

33. Jackson, 1999.

34. Greenfield, 1996.

35. Ibid.

36. Greenfield, 1996.

37. Greenfield, 1996; Jackson, 1999.

38. Jackson, 1999.

39. Greenfield, 1996.

40. Ibid.

41. Ibid., p. 336.

42. Jackson, 1999.

43. Ibid.

44. McNally, 2002.

45. Ibid.

46. Lesh, 2005.

47. Gary Ciocco, "How Dead Beats Became Deadheads: From Emerson and James to Kerouac and Garcia," in Steven Gimbel (Ed.), *The Grateful Dead and Philosophy* 63–74. Peru, IL: Open Court, 2007, p. 71.

48. George-Warren, 1995, p. 28.

Chapter 7

ATTICS OF MY LIFE

My way is music. Music is me being me. . . . I've been into music so
long that I'm dripping with it; it's all I ever expect to do.

—Jerry Garcia quoted in John Rocco,
Dead Reckonings: The Life and Times of the Grateful Dead

More than anything else, Jerry Garcia loved music. Not only was he a
talented and skilled performer, he also knew a great deal about the history
and forms of music. Garcia enjoyed a wide range of musical styles, from
traditional old-time American music and bluegrass to rock, the blues, and
reggae. Across his life, he tried to experience as much music as he could:

> There's a lot of great music in the American experience, and I
> hope to be able to touch as much of it as I can. I feel that I can
> honestly contribute something.[1]

At different times, Garcia referred to himself as a "genre player" and an
"idiom player," much like his father. But Garcia was never locked into one
particular idiom or style of music; instead, he was always exploring new
sounds and approaches:

> You have to get past the idea that music *has* to be *one* thing. To
> be alive in America is to hear all kinds of music constantly—
> radio, records, churches, cats on the street, everywhere music,
> man. And with records, the whole history of music is open to
> everyone who wants to hear it.[2]

In the documentary *Grateful Dawg*, friend David Grisman described Jerry Garcia as an "endless source of imagination." Musician Bruce Hornsby agreed, noting that Garcia was one of the most original guitar players ever. Hornsby explained how Garcia used chromaticism and the five notes of the chromatic scale in interesting ways that were likely influenced by jazz and Garcia's interest in atonalism. Hornsby observed that one of the most distinctive features of Garcia's guitar playing was his sound.[3]

Jerry Garcia seemed to hold a measure of faith that music held and conveyed meaning where other mediums failed, in part because music was deeply spiritual and it preceded and superseded language. Because music was so intertwined in all that he did, Garcia explained his own life in relation to the music he played: "I've always been a musician and into improvising and it's like I consider life to be a continuous series of improvisations."[4]

But music did not necessarily come easily to Garcia. Jerry worked hard and purposefully at being a musician. He was talented, but he knew that talent alone was not enough if he was going to play for public audiences. Garcia practiced long hours every day, often rising before dawn to work on his music. When he was not practicing or rehearsing with one of his groups, he was listening to music others were creating. Some of the music Garcia listened to regularly included Crosby, Stills, and Nash, The Beatles, Traffic, and Neil Young. He sought out music that gave him a particular feel and music that was innovative. Although his own touring and performance schedule were quite intense, there were rare occasions when he was able to take in a concert. For instance, when Bob Marley performed in the United States, Garcia attended one of his first performances.

Of course, Garcia did not just perform music, he created it. Both involved a great deal of effort, and Jerry did not always enjoy the process. He once explained about song writing:

> Well, I don't write them unless I absolutely have to. I don't wake up in the morning and say: "Jeez, I feel great today. I think I'll write a song." I mean, *anything* is more interesting to me than writing a song—"No, I guess I better go feed the cat first." You know what I mean? It's like pulling teeth. I don't enjoy it a bit.[5]

Jerry's long-time writing partner Robert Hunter agreed that writing music is incredibly hard work, and sometimes Jerry was not always motivated to write. Hunter had to push him. Sometimes this involved simply leaving lyrics for Jerry, and then Jerry would put the lyrics to music. Other times writing involved more intense collaboration with the two of them living and working side by side. Jerry found the act of creating a song to be different with each tune. He once explained:

> Sometimes I'll start out with a set of chord changes that're just attractive to my ear. And then I'll hear a sketch of melody over it. Then I'll just sort of let that be around my head for however long it is there, for three or four weeks. I never try to work on stuff, you know, like sit down and labor it . . . then I'll get together with Hunter who writes our lyrics and we'll go through what he's got. If he's got lyrics already written that he likes I'll see if anything first or else we'll start working on something from scratch. But the whole thing is completely organic. I don't have any scheme.[6]

There were times when Hunter created the words and Jerry found a tune almost instantly. This was the case with the song "Casey Jones." Jerry wrote the music in one sitting. "Truckin'" was a different experience altogether, however. Jerry did not think the song flowed well and he had to labor over the music to get the tune just right. In time, "Truckin'" became one of his favorite songs.

Jerry's passion for music sometimes came at great personal cost. Because he cared most about his music, he focused totally on it, often at the expense of those who were around him. He struggled with personal relationships, particularly with women, and some who were closest to him did not consider him to be a good father.[7]

As Garcia struggled with the machine that the Grateful Dead became, the Jerry Garcia Band served as a wonderful release for him. Once he explained that "[t]he Garcia band really reflects my musical personality."[8] Dave Kemper played drums, Melvin Seals was on keyboards, and Jackie LaBranch and Gloria Jones sang back-up vocals. Their main venue was the Warfield in San Francisco, where they played several gigs each month.

Kemper described the Jerry Garcia Band shows as difficult, particularly because the songs were slow and often had the same tempo. Kemper said it was like driving a car with one foot on the gas and the other on the brake pedal.[9] This required a great deal of energy, and each time they played, the tunes were a little different. In spite of the challenges, Kemper loved to play with the band and Jerry. There was a lot of informal improvisation among the band members, and they challenged each other musically throughout each show. Band members knew that they had to be ready if they decided to challenge Jerry, though. Jerry had a lot of chops and could really throw it back to the other players. Nothing ever seemed to phase him. Jerry usually ended each set with an "up" song like "Tangled Up in Blue" because he knew the songs were mostly slower and the audience needed to leave with some energy. The audiences for the Jerry Garcia Band, much like the Deadheads, were instrumental in the performances, and many of them came to the shows because they just wanted to be in the same room with Jerry.

Members of the Jerry Garcia Band explained that Jerry gave everything he had in each show, and they all noted how generous he was, financially and otherwise. Jerry's life was playing his guitar and being onstage, and he loved to give of himself to his music and the audience. Vocalist LaBranch remembered how Jerry was always cool with people. He was known to be a little shy but would always talk to people when they approached him.

Many believed Jerry was a genius, but he was also quite humble. Once Kemper asked Garcia why he didn't write lyrics to songs, and Jerry replied, "Oh man. I've got nothing to say." Kemper explained that Jerry was always careful about what he said because he was uncertain about how people would understand his message. Once Jerry got out of a limo, and a young kid recognized him and asked, "Hey Jerry, how's everything?" Jerry replied, "I don't know man. I haven't tried everything." Later, Jerry told Kemper that he should not have said that. He did not mean to encourage the kid to go out and try everything, and he wondered if that is how the boy would interpret him.[10]

Garcia's band mates appreciated his great sense of humor and sometimes goofy and unique way of viewing experiences in the world. Kemper shared how Jerry once had a bottle of something called "Snake Essence," and he wondered how it tasted. Jerry took a swig, and later laughed that it left a bad taste in his mouth for six weeks.[11]

Over the years, critics would sometimes offer disparaging comments about Garcia's voice. One critic explained that Garcia "couldn't capably carry a tune, which was alright because he couldn't play very well or compose one either."[12] But those who performed with Jerry and his many fans felt otherwise. Robert Hunter explained that Garcia's voice was from the heart and totally unaffected. Members of the Jerry Garcia Band explained that Garcia's voice was real and soulful, and they appreciated how he interpreted and genuinely felt the music he performed. Elvis Costello explained that Jerry sang with the author's voice, that "he just had the right voice for his songs."[13]

Garcia was always a positive person, and he never harbored bad feelings. When he was deep into heroin, he knew that he was making bad decisions for his life, but the drug was one way he escaped from the pressures he felt, particularly with the Grateful Dead. A lot of people depended on him for their livelihood, and it was a huge responsibility to bear.

After his death, Bob Dylan offered perhaps one of the greatest tributes to Jerry as a person and musician:

> There's no way to measure his greatness or magnitude as a person or as a player. I don't think eulogizing will do him justice. He was that great—much more than a superb musician with an uncanny ear and dexterity. He is the very spirit personified of whatever is muddy river country at its core and screams up into the spheres. He really had no equal. To me he wasn't only a musician and friend, he was more like a big brother who taught and showed me more than he'll ever know. There are a lot of spaces and advances between the Carter Family, Buddy Holly and, say, Ornette Coleman, a lot of universes, but he filled them all without being a member of any school. His playing was moody, awesome, sophisticated, hypnotic and subtle. There's no way to convey the loss. It just digs down really deep.[14]

When Jerry Garcia died, he left behind an amazing legacy through his music and art; unfortunately, the personal circumstances of his estate quickly became quite complicated.

NO TOMORROW

At his death, Jerry's estate included the following: $30,000 worth of comic books, $250,000 in musical instruments, various furnishings and computers, art, two cars, a Honda scooter, and royalties and a share of Grateful Dead Productions.[15] Jerry left one-third of his personal property and rights to his wife Deborah, and each of his daughters received one-fifth of his estate. Jerry left 1/10 of his estate to Sunshine Kesey, and another 1/10 to his brother Tiff. He returned the guitars Douglas Irwin made for him to Douglas Irwin. Deborah was named trustee of the will, and while Garcia's financial agreements with Mountain Girl and Manasha were mentioned, albeit vaguely, in the will, Deborah refused to honor those commitments.[16] In 1998, the estate was said to be worth more than $15 million.[17]

Lawsuits and claims against the estate followed, ranging from $980 claimed by Garcia's personal trainer to $15.6 million from Vince DiBiase, who owned some of Garcia's original artwork and the rights to them, a point challenged by Deborah Koons. Manasha Matheson claimed she was owed $3 million due to an agreement she made with Jerry, and John Kahn requested royalties and money for a recording console.[18]

Mountain Girl also filed suit against Koons. Jerry and Mountain Girl signed a statement in 1993 that detailed his financial commitment to Mountain Girl. They did not go to a lawyer or to court to make the statement official. As a result, Mountain Girl had to prove that her relationship with Jerry was based on love, and that she was not seeking his money. During the trial, she read a love letter Jerry wrote to her from a Chicago hotel when he was on tour in the mid-1980s:

> You tickle me with your sweet talk. . . . Your mouth & special secret smiles & the corners of your mouth sweet to touch & kiss & exciting in a tender way. Your incredible eyes that dance & twinkle & flash & flirt & laugh & stun and also warm & soothe & speak of Deepest love. UNBELIEVABLE. I sink into you. I worship you. I love you on every level. EVERY WAY!![19]

He signed the note "your devoted ugly jer," and enclosed money for Mountain Girl and their daughters.

The lawsuit aired on Court TV, something that surprised Mountain Girl. In an interview with David Gans for the *Grateful Dead Hour*, Mountain Girl explained how the entire event seemed to be out of her control and how difficult it was to defend herself, to attend to every word she said. Many who followed the proceedings recognized the irony of attempting to apply middle-class norms to the Grateful Dead's lifestyle.[20] Steve Parish turned the direction of the proceedings by explaining that the Grateful Dead was not a group of conventional people, which meant applying middle-class norms about what a family was or how a family lived would not work.[21] Parish explained to the judge:

> See, we were the Grateful Dead, sir. We were something different. This was an experiment, so we didn't, I didn't, think of things the way you think of things.[22]

In the end, the judge ruled in Mountain Girl's favor.

Even though it was explicit in Garcia's will that his guitars would be returned to Doug Irwin, the Grateful Dead organization argued that Jerry's guitars belonged to them. Phil Lesh did not agree with this claim, and he was distraught by how the members of the Dead were "spinning farther and farther apart" without Jerry's presence.[23] After the lawsuit was settled,

Irwin sold the guitars. Wolf, Jerry's first guitar from Irwin, which he played for six years, brought $700,000. Tiger, the guitar Irwin took six years to build and Garcia played for 11 years, brought $850,000.

In 2005, the Jerry Garcia Estate LLC, a corporation made up of Jerry's beneficiaries, sued Moe's Southwestern Burritos LLC for using Jerry's image and name in their store without permission. While the franchise restaurant used other celebrities names on their products, they created the Alfredo Garcia, a fajita dish, without the Garcia estate's permission, according to charges in the suit. They also allegedly displayed photographs of Jerry in more than 130 stores and in marketing materials.

Keelin Garcia sued Deborah Koons Garcia and the lawyers involved with Jerry's will because she claimed that her money was not distributed properly and Deborah gave poor oversight to Jerry's estate.

Deborah Koons Garcia returned to court in January 2007 because she wished to have rights to unpublished tapes of Jerry performing. Deborah claimed that she wished to professionally restore what she called "The Garcia Tapes," but others involved in the Jerry Garcia Estate LLC were holding up the process. Deborah sued the other members of the corporation.

The legal wrangling over Jerry's estate would no doubt disturb him. Jerry was not a particularly materialistic person and he had a tremendous mistrust of legal systems. When he was asked in an interview approximately two years before he died whether he was concerned about what he would leave behind, Garcia replied:

> No. I'm hoping to leave a clean field—nothing, not a thing. I'm hoping they burn it all with me. I don't feel like there's this body of work that must exist. I'd just as soon take it all with me. There's enough stuff—who needs the clutter, you know? I'd rather have my immortality here while I'm alive. I don't care if it lasts beyond me at all. I'd just as soon it didn't.[24]

Outside Jerry's immediate family and friends, there continues to be an insatiable interest in his possessions and creations. One auction in 2002 brought $23,000 for one of Jerry's leather jackets and $10,000 for his passport. Five years later, an auction of Grateful Dead memorabilia at Bonhams and Butterfields brought high bids for Jerry Garcia's guitars. His 1975 cream-colored Travis Bean guitar sold for $312,000. One of Garcia's acoustic guitars sold for $102,000. A leather guitar strap from 1973 sold for $20,400.[25] Toilets, a dishwasher, stereo cabinets, and other items from Jerry Garcia's Nicasio home were auctioned on the e-Bay Web site in an effort to raise money for the San Francisco–based Sophia Foundation, a nonprofit organization that helps children and families that are going through separations and divorce.

The Jerry Garcia company and the Grateful Dead Productions, which are separate industries, continue to generate several million dollars in revenue each year.[26] Jerry Garcia merchandise sells quite well as the brand extends into new and different markets. In addition to continuing the necktie and Ben & Jerry's ice cream, a new line of wine and rugs were sold with "J.Garcia" as the label.

Displays of Jerry's visual art continued to tour around the country, with support from friends and fellow artists like Mickey Hart and Carlos Santana. In a compilation of Garcia's artwork collected in *Jerry Garcia: The Collected Artwork*, Santana noted:

> Jerry Garcia wasn't a little fish in a little fishbowl: he was the captain of multidimensional navigating. Opening this book, people will have an opportunity to see his multifaceted creativity, how he utilized his energy in many beautiful ways, not just pickin' the guitar.[27]

Those who knew of Jerry's lifelong habit of doodling and drawing share their anecdotes in this book.

AROUND AND AROUND

Garcia's music inspired many artists after his death. A series of tribute bands have been formed over the years. For more than nine years, the Dark Star Orchestra has performed across the country, recreating Grateful Dead shows. The group is quite popular, logging more than 1,500 performances. Sometimes former Grateful Dead members, including Bob Weir and Donna Godchaux, join the Dark Star Orchestra on stage. The band's commitment to "raising the Dead" has earned praises from *Rolling Stone* magazine and other critics.

Boris Garcia is another tribute band, a bluegrass band in the form of Old and in the Way. Dennis McNally enthusiastically endorsed the band, praising their unique sound and excellent songwriting. One member of Boris Garcia, Bob Stirner, formerly was a member of another Grateful Dead tribute band called Living Earth.

Ten years after Garcia's death, the Detroit rapper Proof dedicated an album to the Grateful Dead. The album, which climbed to number 65 on the Billboard 200 chart, was named *Searching for Jerry Garcia*. The album included guest artists like 50 Cent, MC Breed, Rude Jude, and Method Man, but no Grateful Dead or Jerry Garcia tunes.

The year 2008 brought Jerry Garcia and the Grateful Dead's music to new and different audiences. The remaining members of the Grateful Dead and the Allman Brothers performed concerts on behalf of the Barack Obama presidential campaign. Grateful Dead fans who were accustomed to the apolitical nature of the band were surprised to see the group offer political support for a presidential candidate, and some claimed on various Web sites that Jerry Garcia would have never agreed to this.

In April 2008 Mickey Hart and Bob Weir announced that the Grateful Dead archives would be donated to the University of California, Santa Cruz. The general public and academic researchers would have access to the archives in a room called "Dead Centre." Included among the archives are business records, photographs, posters, press clips, and other memorabilia. It is anticipated that thousands of people from all over the world will visit the archive.

Six Grateful Dead songs were made available on the popular video game Rock Band: "China Cat Sunflower," "Casey Jones," "Sugar Magnolia," "Truckin'," "Franklin's Tower," and "I Need a Miracle." Lee Johnson, an American composer, released an orchestral version of the Grateful Dead's music titled "Dead Symphony." Johnson, who was not a Deadhead, arranged the music over a 10-year period. It was recorded with the Russian National Symphony. A live performance with the Baltimore Symphony Orchestra was given on August 1, 2008, what would have been Garcia's 66th birthday. Johnson explained that Garcia's music clearly was created by a master craftsman.

Further tributes took different forms. A 600-seat amphitheater at 40 John F. Shelley Drive in San Francisco was named in Jerry Garcia's honor on the 10th anniversary of his death. Jerry Day is celebrated every year since 2002 on the anniversary of Jerry Garcia's birthday. The Crocker-Amazon playground, near Jerry's first childhood home on Amazon Street in San Francisco, was renovated in 2002 with Garcia's art.

The Internet perpetuates ongoing attention to Garcia, including posthumous communication with him. On one Web site, bloggers create dialogue with Garcia in the afterlife. Here Jerry reports that his time in the afterlife has been "pretty far out," but he goes on to lament that "we don't get many new tunes up here, man."[28] Similarly, Wendy Weir, Bob Weir's sister, recorded her channeling efforts to reach what she calls Jerry's Oversoul to find out how Jerry's life purpose can be fulfilled.[29] The message from Jerry to the band is simple: keep making music.

DREAM ME A DREAM OF MY OWN

In 2003, *Rolling Stone* magazine released its list of the 100 best guitar players. Garcia was 13th. He was known for his ability to take risks, to create dynamic melodic leads, to move from finger picking to flat picking, and to create so-called teases (transposing pieces of one song within another song). He remains famous as the leader of a cultural phenomenon known for challenging norms and engaging in unconventional practices.

After Garcia's death, in an interview with Blair Jackson, Robert Hunter explained how Jerry had a depth of soul to express through his music, that he could express so much and was brilliant in so many directions. Hunter knew from firsthand experience that Jerry worked hard at what he did. From a young age, Garcia knew that he wanted to play guitar, to spend his life with music, and he worked endlessly every day to accomplish that goal. Garcia ran scales, studied music, and practiced countless hours alone and with members of his bands. His advice to guitar players was:

> You can't avoid finding your own voice if you keep playing. You have a voice, whether you recognize it or not. There are certain things you can't escape, like your own nervous system. It provides things like the rate of vibrato you're capable of performing, which is almost a nervous reaction. The only danger is falling too much in love with guitar playing. The music is the most important thing, and the guitar is only the instrument.[30]

NOTES

1. Holly George-Warren, *Garcia: By the Editors of The Rolling Stone*. New York: Little Brown and Company, 1995, p. 196.

2. Ibid., p. 64.

3. Blair Jackson, *Garcia: An American Life*. New York: The Penguin Group, 1999

4. Jerry Garcia, Charles Reich, and Jann Wenner, *Garcia: A Signpost to a New Space*. New York: De Capo Press, 1972, p. 20.

5. John Rocco, *Dead Reckonings: The Life and Times of the Grateful Dead*. New York: Schirmer Books, 1999, p. 249.

6. Garcia, Reich, and Wenner, 1972, pp. 51–52.

7. Robert Greenfield, *Dark Star*. New York: William Morrow and Company, 1996.

8. George-Warren, 1995, p. 196.

9. Barry Smolin, "Drumming At The Edge of Jerry: An Interview with David Kemper," http://www.well.com/user/shmo/kemper.html (accessed November 29, 2008).

10. Information from Dave Kemper as told in the documentary *Jerry Garcia Band: Live at the Shoreline* (1990).

11. Ibid.

12. Robert G. Weiner (Ed.), *Perspectives on the Grateful Dead: Critical Writings*. Westport, CT: Greenwood Press, 1999, p. xx.

13. George-Warren, 1995, n.p.

14. Ibid., p. 30.

15. Dennis McNally, *A Long Strange Trip*. New York: Broadway Books, 2002.

16. David Gans, "Carolyn Garcia interview" (1997), http://www.levity.com/gans/MGinterview.html (accessed September 1, 2008).

17. Nancy Isles Nation, "Jerry Garcia's Daughter Sues over Distribution of His Estate," *Oakland Tribune*, http://findarticles.com/p/articles/mi_qn4176/is_20070101/ai_n17087046 (accessed November 29, 2008).

18. Jackson, 1999.

19. Donna Horowitz, "Love Light Shines in Jerry Garcia Estate Trial," *SF Gate*, http://www.sfgate.com/cgi-bin/article.cgi?f=/e/a/1996/12/12/NEWS8420.dtl&hw=Mountain+Girl+Garcia&sn=005&sc=659 (accessed November 29, 2008).

20. David Fraser and Vaughan Black, "Legally Dead: The Grateful Dead and American Legal Culture," in Robert G. Weiner (Ed.), *Perspectives on the Grateful Dead: Critical Writings*. Westport, CT: Greenwood Press, 1999.

21. "Carolyn Garcia Interview by David Gans," http://www.levity.com/gans/MGinterview.html (accessed November 29, 2008).

22. David Fraser and Vaughan Black, 1999, p. 20.

23. Phil Lesh, *Searching for the Sound*. New York: Little Brown and Company, 2005, p. 328.

24. George-Warren, 1995, p. 197.

25. "Jerry Garcia's Travis Bean Guitar Fetches $312,000," press release, *Modern Guitars Magazine*, http://www.modernguitars.com/archives/003245.html (accessed November 29, 2008).

26. Seth Schiesel, "Jerry Garcia: The Man, the Myth, the Area Rug," *New York Times*, http://www.nytimes.com/2005/08/09/national/09dead.html (accessed November 29, 2008).

27. April Higashi, *Jerry Garcia: The Collected Artwork*. New York: Thunders Mouth Press, 2005, p. xxi.

28. Jesse Jarnow, "Forty Years Upon Our Heads," *Perfect Sound Forever Online Music Magazine*, http://www.furious.com/PERFECT/jerrygarciadead.html (accessed November 29, 2008).

29. Wendy Weir, In the Spirit: Conversations with the Spirit of Jerry Garcia. New York: Three Rivers Press, 2000.

30. Jon Sievert, "Remembering the Music, Vibe, and Guitars of Jerry Garcia," *Guitar Player Online Edition*, http://www.guitarplayer.com/article/remembering-the-music/Nov-05/15094 (accessed November 29, 2008).

GLOSSARY OF KEY PEOPLE AND TERMS

The Acid Tests—These were a series of parties hosted by Ken Kesey in the 1960s where people experimented with and freely used LSD, otherwise known as acid. The Warlocks, renamed the Grateful Dead, were the house band for these parties.

Anarchy—Garcia tended to use this complex and often ambiguous term to mean a spontaneous order. He did not believe in dictatorship or having leaders because he felt this would result in constraints rather than creativity.[1]

Beatniks (aka Beats)—To the Beats, "the writer is not only defined as one who creates art, but rather the life of the writer itself can become the art."[2] Beats were known to "talk fast, live faster, and ask questions later."[3]

Cassady, Neal (1926–1968)—Cassady was the inspiration for the character Dean Moriarty in Jack Kerouac's book *On the Road*. He became a symbol of the Beat generation and was good friends with members of the Grateful Dead.

Deadheads—These are Grateful Dead fans known for their intense loyalty and sense of community. Typical fans were white, male, and middle class, but fans came from all walks of life. Famous Deadheads include basketball player Bill Walton, professional basketball coach Phil Jackson, Owen Chamberlain (a Nobel laureate in physics), artist Keith Haring, Senator Patrick Leahy of Vermont, and mythologist Joseph Campbell.

Diggers—This was group who lived in San Francisco during the 1960s and advocated for free identity, free families, and free myths.

Ginsberg, Allen (1926–1997)—Ginsberg was an American poet best known for his poem *Howl*, which is biographical and a historical account of the Beat generation. He was an activist, a beatnik, and a prolific writer. Ginsberg won the National Book Award in 1973 for his book *The Fall of America*. Many of the poems in this collection condemned the United States for its involvement in Vietnam.

Haight-Ashbury—This is a district in the city of San Francisco, often referred to as "the Haight." It is named for the intersection of Haight and Ashbury Streets. The neighborhood became famous as the geographic center for hippies in the 1960s. The Grateful Dead had an office and many lived at 710 Ashbury Street in the mid to late 1960s.

Hammond B-3 organ—The Hammond B-3 is an electric organ widely used in progressive rock bands in the 1960s and 1970s including Procol Harem, Pink Floyd, and Emerson, Lake and Palmer. Tom Constanten introduced this instrument to the band when he joined in 1968, and Brent Mydland continued to perform on a B-3 through the 1980s.

Jug band—This is a band that includes a jug player, who buzzes his or her lips into the top of a ceramic jug, and a mixture of traditional and home-made instruments. Jug bands could include guitar, banjo, and mandolin, as well as a washboard, tub, spoons, and kazoo.

Kerouac, Jack (1922–1969)—Kerouac was an American author best known for his book *On the Road*. He is among the best known writers of the Beat generation. His work inspired other writers including Hunter S. Thompson and Ken Kesey, as well as musicians like The Beatles, Bob Dylan, and Jerry Garcia.

Nitrous oxide—This is a chemical compound most commonly known as laughing gas. The Grateful Dead recorded "What's Become of Baby" while using nitrous oxide.

Psychedelic drugs—These drugs alter the thought processes and perceptions of the mind. They are part of a wider class of drugs known as hallucinogens.

The Rex Foundation—This is a philanthropic organization founded by members of the Grateful Dead to support creative efforts in the arts, music, and education. Since 1984, the organization has provided more than $8 million to over 1,000 recipients.[4]

Vox continental organ—Pigpen played this organ during the early days of the Grateful Dead. Introduced in 1962, the black and white keys were reversed from regular keyboards.[5]

NOTES

1. For more on Garcia's views on anarchy, see Horace Fairlamb, "Community at the Edge of Chaos: The Dead's Cultural Revolution," in Steven Gimbel (Ed.), *The Grateful Dead and Philosophy*. Peru, IL: Open Court Publishing, pp. 13–26, 2007.

2. Gary Ciocco, "How Dead Beats Became Deadheads: From Emerson and James to Kerouac and Garcia," in Steven Gimbel (Ed.), *The Grateful Dead and Philosophy*. Peru, IL: Open Court, 2007, p. 66.

3. Ibid., p. 69.

4. Rex Foundation, http://www.rexfoundation.org (accessed November 29, 2008).

5. Nostalgia, "Vox Continental," http://www.hollowsun.com/vintage/vox_conti/index.html (accessed November 29, 2008).

Appendix 1

WHERE ARE THEY NOW? THE LIVING MEMBERS OF THE DEAD AND FRIENDS

John Barlow is a founding member of the Electric Frontier Foundation (EFF), a nonprofit organization dedicated to preserving free speech rights in the context of the digital age. He currently serves as vice chairman of EFF's board of directors. Barlow is also a fellow with the Berkman Center for Internet and Society at Harvard Law School, and he is a member of the International Academy of Digital Arts and Sciences.

Tom Constanten released several albums in the 1990s. He performed keyboards with several groups since leaving the Grateful Dead, including Jefferson Starship, which evolved from the 1960s band Jefferson Airplane, as well as with Grateful Dead tribute bands like Terrapin Flyer. He resides in Charlotte, North Carolina.

Deborah Koons Garcia is a filmmaker. In 2004 she directed a film titled *The Future of Food*. She lives in Marin County, California.

Manasha Matheson Garcia took Jerry's last name, even though they never married. As of 1996, she was running a music production company called Say Grace Music. Little has been reported on Manasha since 1996.

Mountain Girl Garcia is an active member of the board for the Rex Foundation as well as a member of the advisory board for the Marijuana Policy Project, an organization advocating for change from prohibition of marijuana to a system with reasonable regulation of its use, including use by terminally ill patients. Mountain Girl resides in Oregon with her husband, William Burrell.

Sara Ruppenthal Garcia was involved with clinical health psychology, and when the book *Dark Star* was published she was beginning a postdoctoral fellowship in this area.

Tiff Garcia lives in Novato California where he enjoys guitars and producing artwork. He sells limited edition lithographs of his brother's artwork.

Trixie Garcia is a painter who lives in the San Francisco Bay area.

Annabelle Garcia-McLean lives near Eugene, Oregon. She is a painter and with her husband, Scott, co-owns an independent record label called Leisure King Records.

Donna Godchaux is still performing as a singer, primarily with the group Donna Jean and the Tricksters. She occasionally appears with Bob Weir and Ratdog as well as Dark Star Orchestra. She resides in Alabama.

David Grisman continues to perform with the David Grisman Quintet (founded in 1975) as well as with the David Grisman Bluegrass Experience (DGBX).

Mickey Hart remains immersed in the study of percussion from around the world and global music traditions. He performs with Planet Drumz, the Rhythm Devils (which feature new songs written by Robert Hunter), and the Mickey Hart Band. More information can be found at: http://www.mickeyhart.net/home/

Robert Hunter continues to write music and occasionally performs publicly as a solo acoustic guitarist.

Sunshine Kesey is a glass artist and instructor at the Eugene Glass School, a nonprofit organization in Eugene, Oregon.

Bill Kreutzmann performs with a number of acts, including Mickey Hart in the Rhythm Devils. He also works as a visual artist.

Phil Lesh administers a charitable organization, the Unbroken Chain Foundation, with his wife Jill. Phil underwent liver transplant surgery in 1998, and he is currently a prostate cancer survivor. Phil performs regularly with the group Phil Lesh and Friends, and his public performances often include his sons Grahame and Brian. More information can be found at: http://www.phillesh.net/

Barbara Meier continues to be a poet and painter. She lives in New Mexico.

Ron Rakow was sentenced to five years in prison in April 2007 for tax evasion. He owed the Internal Revenue Service $2.2 million for hiding assets beginning in 1985.

Melvin Seals continues to play electric organ with The Jerry Garcia Band, whose mission is to continue the musical legacy of Jerry Garcia. Information on The Jerry Garcia Band can be found here: http://www.jgbband.com/blog/

Bob Weir remains on the board for the Rex Foundation and is an honorary member of the board of directors for the Rainforest Action Network. He performs regularly with his band Ratdog, as well as reunions of living Grateful Dead band members. More information can be found at: http://www.rat-dog.com/

Appendix 2

JERRY GARCIA'S GUITARS

This list is based on information from "A Pictoral Guide to the Guitars Played by Jerry Garcia" (found at http://www.nii.net/~obie1/deadcd/garcia_guitars.htm), and "Jerry Garcia Guitar History" (found at http://www.dozin.com/jers/guitar/history.htm#). The guitars are listed in the order that Garcia acquired them.

Danelectro guitar—Garcia's first guitar, a gift for his 15th birthday.

Stella 12-string—Garcia played this guitar in the early 1960s when he was playing American folksongs and Appalachian ballads at Kepler's in Palo Alto. Leadbelly also played a Stella 12-string.

Guild Starfire—Garcia played this guitar, which was red, in the early years of the Warlocks and the Grateful Dead, switching to the Gibson SG Les Paul sometime in 1968. He played a Guild Starfire on the Grateful Dead's first album.

Gibson Les Paul—Beginning in 1969, Garcia switched between this guitar and the Gibson SG Les Paul.

Gibson SG Les Paul—Garcia switched from the Guild Starfire to this guitar in 1968. This is associated with the "Live/Dead" sound and had a Vox Crybaby wah-wah.

Sunburst Strat—Jerry played this guitar in 1970. It had a Brazilian Rosewood fingerboard.

Martin D-18—This is the guitar Jerry played at Woodstock and on the albums *American Beauty* and *Workingman's Dead*.

ZB Pedal Steel Guitar—Garcia taught himself to play the pedal steel guitar, largely through experimentation. He played this instrument in the Dead song "Cosmic Charlie," as well as with Crosby, Stills, and Nash on their song "Teach Your Children Well."

Alembic—One of the first custom-built guitars Jerry played (around 1971).

Fender Stratocaster—aka "The Alligator." A guitar with a natural finish given to Garcia by Graham Nash. The guitar had an alligator sticker on it.

Travis Bean—An aluminum-neck guitar designed by Travis Bean from southern California.

Wolf—A custom-designed guitar Garcia played beginning in 1973. It was designed by Doug Irwin and had a wolf inlay.

Tiger—The second custom-made guitar from Irwin. Garcia played this guitar for 11 years, beginning in 1979. In addition to the tiger inlay on the front of the guitar, there is a curly maple plate on the back inlaid with a mother-of-pearl and abalone art nouveau flower. Garcia played this guitar during his last concert. Lightning-Bolt was getting a new bridge, and he experienced problems with Rosebud, so he returned to this guitar to finish the show.

Takamine acoustic—This is the guitar Jerry used in acoustic sets in the 1980s.

Rosebud—This is the third custom-built guitar from Doug Irwin. Garcia began to play this guitar in 1989. It cost $11,000 and had a dancing skeleton holding a red rose on the front ebony cover plate.

Alvarez-Yairi—This is the guitar Garcia used during live shows with his friend David Grisman.

Lightning-Bolt—A guitar made for Garcia by Florida woodworker Stephen Cripe. Jerry began to play this guitar in 1993. Garcia declared that this was the guitar he had been waiting for and began to play it exclusively. In April 1995, Garcia commissioned a second guitar from Cripe called "Top Hat."

Appendix 3

INTERESTING FACTS ABOUT SONGS JERRY GARCIA ROUTINELY PERFORMED

"The Other One" was part of the Grateful Dead's repertoire for longer than any other song they performed, from 1967 to their next-to-last show in 1995.[1]

"Born Cross-Eyed" is one of Bob Weir's first compositions and is a nod to his own struggles with strabismus, a condition that causes a person's eyes to be misaligned.

"Alligator" is the first song lyricist Robert Hunter wrote for the Grateful Dead.

"St. Stephen" is one of the most symbolic of the Grateful Dead's songs. It has little to do with the original St. Stephen (the Christian martyr who died in 34 a.d.); instead the song is one of a search for higher truth.

"Dark Star" is one of the most famous songs by the Grateful Dead. Jerry Garcia and Bob Weir improvised extensively in this piece, which once stretched to 48 minutes during a performance in Rotterdam in 1972. Hunter's lyrics are profound, inspired in part by the poet T. S. Eliot's work in *The Love Song of J Alfred Prufrock*.

"New Speedway Boogie" was written after the tragic events at the Altamont concert in 1969. Robert Hunter's lyrics served as a retort to a newspaper article written about the event.

"Cumberland Blues" is based on Appalachian musical traditions. It tells about the difficult life of miners.

"Casey Jones," one of the most popular and recognizable Grateful Dead songs, relays the story of an Illinois-Central train wreck that occurred in April 1900. The Hunter/Garcia lyrics intertwine facts from the actual event with their own version of the story.

"Box of Rain" is one of the best Grateful Dead songs written by Phil Lesh. The song was written as Lesh's father was dying of cancer.

"Friend of the Devil" tells the tale of a vagabond who barters with the Devil. The song was originally written when Robert Hunter was affiliated with New Riders of the Purple Sage, and fellow New Rider John Dawson collaborated with Garcia and Hunter on the song. Hunter later said that this is the closest he and Jerry came to writing a classic song.

"Sugar Magnolia" is a Hunter/Weir collaboration that was performed at more live concerts than any other original Grateful Dead tune. The song is a playful, carefree song about being stupid and in love.

"Ripple" is one of the Grateful Dead's most recognizable songs. In addition to playing the song at Grateful Dead concerts, Garcia played Ripple in 70 of his own concerts between 1982 and 1992. Hunter wrote the lyrics while traveling with the Grateful Dead in London in 1970.

"Truckin'" is an autobiographical song that tells the band's experiences on the road in the early 1970s, including the drug bust in New Orleans. Garcia once explained that they expected to keep adding verses to the song as the band continued to tour. The song's line "what a long strange trip it's been" is perhaps one of the most famous Hunter wrote, symbolizing much in relation to the Grateful Dead.

"Bird Song" was a Hunter/Garcia song written as a tribute to Janis Joplin after her untimely death.

"Mexicali Blues" marked the first collaboration between John Barlow and Bob Weir. The song was written in Middletown, Connecticut.

"Cassidy" was written as a tribute to Neal Cassady. It is a biographical song written by Weir and Barlow. A sentimental favorite among the Deadheads, the song was played more than 300 times in live concerts, including the Dead's third-to-last show in 1995.

"Brown-Eyed Women" is the Grateful Dead's American folktale that tells the story of a bootlegger and his family during the Prohibition and Great Depression. The Dead performed this song nearly 350 times in live concerts.

"Stella Blue" is a Hunter/Garcia ballad likely inspired by Stella guitars, played by famous blues musicians like Leadbelly.

"Terrapin Station" is a Hunter/Garcia collaboration. Hunter claimed to write the lyrics while looking at the San Francisco Bay from a window during a lightning storm. Garcia was supposedly driving in the same storm, and turned around to return home to write down the music that was in his head. The next day, the two met and their respective work was put together in this song.

"Alabama Getaway" gives the state of Alabama the distinction of being the third state to appear in a Grateful Dead title. It reflects the "home churned country" music that the Grateful Dead could play.

"Touch of Grey" became the Grateful Dead's anthem of survival. Hunter wrote the lyrics in England, but the song took on significant meaning to fans after Garcia's recovery from a diabetic coma. Garcia's "I will survive" brought rousing cheers from the audience. The song was the Grateful Dead's first to crack the top 40, and its first top 10 hit, climbing the charts to number 8.

NOTE

1. The information in this appendix is paraphrased from Stephen Peters, *Grateful Dead; What a Long, Strange Trip: The Stories Behind Every Song 1965–1995*. New York: Thunder's Mouth Press, 1999.

SELECTED BIBLIOGRAPHY

Avlon, Jack. "Jerry Garcia's Conservative Children" (2005). *New York Sun*. Available at http://www.nysun.com/article/18288. Accessed December 11, 2007.

Bonham and Butterfields. "Press release" (2007). Available at http://www.modern guitars.com/archives/003245.html. Accessed September 1, 2008.

Carson, Rachel. *Silent Spring*. New York: Houghton Mifflin, 1962.

Ciocco, Gary. "How Dead Beats Became Deadheads: From Emerson and James to Kerouac and Garcia." In Gimbel, S. (Ed.), *The Grateful Dead and Philosophy*, pp. 63–74. Peru, IL: Open Court Publishing, 2007.

Decurtis, Anthony. "Jerry Garcia: The Rolling Stone Interview. The Music Never Stops." *Rolling Stone* (1993). Available at http://www.rollingstone.com/news/story/7539574/the_music_never_stops. Accessed August 29, 2008.

Dodd, David, and Diane Spaulding. *The Grateful Dead Reader*. London: Oxford University Press, 2000.

Fairlamb, Horace. "Community at the Edge of Chaos: The Dead's Cultural Revolution." In Gimbel, S. (Ed.), *The Grateful Dead and Philosophy*, pp. 13–26. Peru, IL: Open Court Publishing, 2007.

Fraser, David, and Vaughn Black. "Legally Dead: The Grateful Dead and American Legal Culture." In Weiner, Robert (Ed.), *Perspectives on the Grateful Dead: Critical Writings*, pp. 19–39. Westport, CT: Greenwood Press, 1999.

Freidan, Betty. *The Feminine Mystique*. New York: W.W. Norton and Company, 1963.

Gans, David. "Carolyn Garcia interview" (1997). Available at http://www.levity.com/gans/MGinterview.html. Accessed September 1, 2008.

Garcia, Jerry. *Harrington Street*. New York: Delacourt Press, 1995.

Garcia, Jerry, Charles Reich, and Jann Wenner. *Garcia: A Signpost to a New Space*. New York: De Capo Press, 1972.

Gass, Paul. "Buddhism through the eyes of the Dead." In Gimbel, S. (Ed.), *The Grateful Dead and Philosophy*, pp. 127–37. Peru, IL: Open Court Publishing, 2007.

George-Warren, Holly. *Garcia: By the Editors of the Rolling Stone*. New York: Little, Brown and Company, 1995.

Gimbel, Steven (Ed.). *The Grateful Dead and Philosophy*. Peru, IL: Open Court Publishing, 2007.

Greenfield, Robert. *Dark Star*. New York: William Morrow and Company, 1996.

Gura, Philip, and James Bollman. *America's Instrument: The Banjo in the Nineteenth Century*. Chapel Hill: University of North Carolina Press, 1999.

Hiatt, Brian. "Monterey Pop." *Rolling Stone* 1030/1031 (2007), 93–94.

Higashi, April. *Jerry Garcia: The Collected Artwork*. New York: Thunders Mouth Press, 2005.

Horowitz, Donna. "Love Light Shines in Jerry Garcia Estate Trial: "Mountain Girl" Reads Grateful Dead Guitarist's Sugary Letter" (1996). Available at http://www.sfgate.com/cgi-bin/article.cgi?f=/e/a/1996/12/12/NEWS8420.dtl&hw=Mountain+Girl+Garcia&sn=005&sc=659. Accessed October 12, 2008.

Horowitz, Donna. "Daddy Garcia: Despite His Advice to Do Drugs, Jerry's Daughters Say They Have Rejected Their Father's Hippie Lifestyle" (1996). SF Gate. Available at http://www.sfchroniclemarketplace.com/cgi-bin/article.cgi?f=/e/a/1996/12/26/NEWS9534.dtl&hw=annabelle+garcia&sn=007&sc=589. Accessed October 10, 2008.

Huxley, Aldous. *The Doors of Perception and Heaven and Hell*. New York: Harper Collins, 1954.

Jackson, Blair. "Another Time's Forgotten Space" (2001). Available at http://www.blairjackson.com/chapter_one_additions.htm. Accessed July 2, 2008.

Jackson, Blair. *Garcia: An American Life*. New York: The Penguin Group, 1999.

Jarnow, Jesse. "A Recent 'From Beyond' Rap with Jerry Garcia" (2006). *Perfect Sound Forever Online Music Magazine*. Available at http://www.furious.com/PERFECT/jerrygarciadead.html. Accessed September 1, 2008.

Kaiser, Henry. "Jerry Garcia Live" (2007). *Guitar Players Online Edition*. Available at http://www.guitarplayer.com/article/jerry-garcia-live/oct-07/32077. Accessed December 11, 2007.

Lee, Martin, and Bruce Shlain. *Acid Dreams: The Complete Social History of LSD: The CIA, the Sixties, and Beyond*. New York: Grove Press, 1985.

Lesh, Phil. *Searching for the Sound*. New York: Little Brown & Company, 2005.

Marre, Jeremy. *The Grateful Dead: Anthem to Beauty*. New York: Eagle Rock Entertainment, 1997.

McNally, Dennis. *A Long Strange Trip*. Broadway Books: New York, 2002.

Nation, Nancy. "Jerry Garcia's Daughter Sues Over Distribution of His Estate" (2007). Available at http://findarticles.com/p/articles/mi_qn4176/is_20070101/ai_n17087046. Accessed September 1, 2008.

Pelovitz, David. "No, but I've Been to Shows: Accepting the Dead and Rejecting the Deadheads." In Weiner, R. (Ed.), *Perspectives on the Grateful Dead: Critical Writings*, pp. 55–77. Westport, CT: Greenwood Press, 1999.

Peters, Stephen. Grateful Dead; *What a Long, Strange Trip: The Stories Behind Every Song 1965–1995*. New York: Thunder's Mouth Press, 1999.

Reisch, George, and Matthew Turner. "Freedom's Just Another Word for Nothing Left to Choose" (2007). Available at http://www.popmatters.com/pm/column/43447/freedoms-just-another-word-for-nothing-left-to-choose/. Accessed July 2, 2008.

Rocco, John. *Dead Reckonings: The Life and Times of the Grateful Dead*. New York: Schirmer Books, 1999.

Schiesel, Seth. "Jerry Garcia: The Man, the Myth, the Area Rug" (2005). *New York Times*. Available at http://www.nytimes.com/2005/08/09/national/09dead.html?pagewanted=1&_r=3. Accessed September 1, 2008.

Selvin, Joel. "Summer of Love: 40 Years Later/Julia Brigden (Girl Freiberg)" (2007). SF Gate. Available at http://www.sfgate.com/cgi-bin/article.cgi?f=/c/a/2007/05/20/MNSOLBRIGDEN20.DTL. Accessed July 2, 2008.

Selvin, Joel. "Summer of Love: 40 Years Later/Carolyn Garcia (Mountain Girl)" (2007). SF Gate. Available at http://www.sfgate.com/cgi-bin/article.cgi?f=/c/a/2007/05/20/MNSOLGARCIA20.DTL. Accessed July 2, 2008.

Sievert, John. "Remembering the Music, Vibe, and Guitars of Jerry Garcia" (2005). *Guitar Player Online Edition*. Accessed at http://www.guitarplayer.com/article/remembering-the-music/Nov-05/15094. Accessed November 24, 2007.

Simon, Scott. "Composer Introduces a 'Dead' Symphony" (2008). National Public Radio. Available at http://www.npr.org/templates/story/story.php?storyId=92932316. Accessed September 1, 2008.

Vonnegut, Kurt. *The Sirens of Titan*. New York: The Dial Press, 1959.

Weiner, Robert (Ed.). *Perspectives on the Grateful Dead: Critical Writings*. Westport, CT: Greenwood Press, 1999.

Weir, Wendy. *In the Spirit: Conversations with the Spirit of Jerry Garcia*. New York: Three Rivers Press, 2000.

INDEX

About the Author

JACQUELINE EDMONDSON is Associate Professor of Education at Pennsylvania State University. She teaches undergraduate and graduate courses in language and literacy education. She is the author of *Jesse Owens: A Biography* (2007), *Condoleezza Rice: A Biography* (2006), and *Venus and Serena Williams: A Biography* (2005).